The Publisher wishes to thank **Ikea Pte Ltd**, Malaysia; **Remix Home Shoppe Sdn Bhd**, Malaysia; and **Royel Ampang Point**, Malaysia for the loan of their crockery and utensils.

Chef	:	Don Yong
Project Editor/Editor of Malay Edition	:	Jamilah Mohd Hassan
Art Direction/Designer	:	Christopher Wong
Photographer	:	Edmond Ho
Editor of English Edition	:	Lydia Leong
Project Co-ordinator	:	Christine Chong
Production Co-ordinator	:	Nor Sidah Haron

© 2003 Times Media Private Limited

Published by Times Editions
An imprint of Times Media Private Limited
A member of the Times Publishing Group

Times Centre, 1 New Industrial Road, Singapore 536196
Tel: (65) 6213 9288   Fax: (65) 6285 4871
E-mail: te@tpl.com.sg
Online Book Store: http://www.timesone.com.sg/te

Times Subang, Lot 46 Subang Hi-Tech Industrial Park
Batu Tiga, 40000 Shah Alam, Selangor Darul Ehsan, Malaysia
Tel & Fax: (603) 5636 3517   E-mail: cchong@tpg.com.my

National Library Board (Singapore) Cataloguing in Publication Data

Yong, Don.
    Bread winners / [chef, Don Yong]. – Singapore : Times Editions, c2003.
    p. cm. – (Celebrity chefs' cookbooks)
    ISBN : 981-232-205-1

1. Bread.   2. Cookery (Bread)   I. Title.   II. Series: Celebrity chefs' cookbooks

    TX769
    641.815 – dc21   SLS2002045436

Printed by Times Printers Pte Ltd

To my dearest mother

Contents

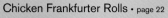

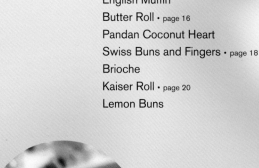

There are few aromas as wonderful as that of baked bread. The excitement of mixing the dough, the satisfaction of seeing it rise and the feeling of joy when seeing and smelling the golden loaves as they emerge from the oven is beyond description. Of course, the ultimate enjoyment is the first taste of the bread you have baked.

This book is written for those with a keen interest in baking. It is also designed for baking school students who will need to learn about bread and fermented goods as part of their course in baking, catering and domestic science. It would also be of great value to the practising baker and chef.

The aim of this book is to simplify the art of bread making, so that it becomes both fun and enjoyable. Popular ethnic products such as steamed pau, roti canai, chapati and fried Chinese doughnut are also included for variety.

Making bread is easy once you understand the functions of the ingredients and the processes. The four essential ingredients used are flour, yeast, salt and water. Other ingredients such as butter, eggs, milk powder and sugar may be added to impart good aroma, flavour, softness, colour and improved texture to the bread.

It is necessary to use high protein flour, strong flour or bread flour in order to produce a good loaf of bread. The protein (gluten) in the flour provides structure to the dough, creating a loaf with good volume. To further enhance the volume and texture of bread, most modern bakers supplement the dough with bread improvers. These are mainly oxidising agents or strengtheners. In using these improvers, the softness and shelf life of the bread is also improved.

Yeast is the leavening agent in breads. It ferments sugars, creating carbon dioxide, acids and other flavourful substances that impart a wonderful flavour and aroma to the bread. The yeast used in this book is instant dry yeast. It comes sealed in vacuum-packed sachets, and can be kept for up to a year if unopened. Once opened, it should be consumed within a week. Fresh yeast (compressed yeast) gives better gassing powder. If fresh yeast is used, increase the amount by 2–3 times that of instant yeast.

Salt is another important ingredient in bread making. It enhances the flavour of the bread while controlling fermentation and strengthening the gluten, making it more extensible.

Water helps to moisten the protein in flour so that gluten can be formed. It is also very important in controlling the dough temperature. The desired dough temperature should fall between 27°C and 30°C. A dough temperature above 30°C will result in bread with poor texture, low volume and a coarser grain. To achieve the ideal dough temperature, regulate the water temperature based on the room and flour temperature and the amount of heat generated during mixing. Generally, if you are mixing the dough on a warm day (30°C), the water used should be cold (5°C). On the other hand, if the room temperature falls to 16°C and below, warm water just above 30°C is required.

The technology of bread making is basically in the mixing. During mixing, liquid is added to the dry ingredients to develop the dough. The best way to check whether the dough is fully developed is by the stretch test. Stretch a small piece of dough with your fingers. If the dough can be stretched into a thin translucent film without breaking, it is fully developed.

The next important stage after mixing is fermentation. The dough is matured when it has doubled in size. The proving temperature is best maintained at around 37°C. If a bread proving unit is not available, the dough must be placed in an airtight container or plastic bag and left in a warm place. If the place is not warm enough, you may need to double the proving time. A simple test to check if the dough is fully proved, is to press the surface of the dough lightly with your fingers. If the dough springs back slowly, it is fully proved.

There are several methods of bread making. The best quality bread in terms of aroma, flavour, softness and keeping quality is produced by the sponge and dough method and it is used extensively in this book. I have also included helpful hints and ideas at the end of each recipe to provide advice on producing quality baked products. I hope you enjoy using these recipes as much as I enjoyed writing this book.

DON YONG

Croissant

Ingredients:

Plain flour (all-purpose flour)	100 g
Strong white flour (bread flour)	400 g
Milk powder	20 g
Bread improver	8 g
Instant dry yeast	10 g
Sugar	50 g
Salt	10 g
Egg	25 g (½, small)
Cold water	225 g
Butter	40 g, softened
Butter	225 g, firm

Method:

- With an electric mixer and dough hook at low speed, blend the ingredients (except firm butter) for 6 minutes. Round up the dough and allow it to relax on a flour-dusted work surface for 20 minutes. Roll it out into a rectangular shape (length twice as long as the breadth) about 1-cm thick.

- Transfer the dough onto a tray and wrap with plastic. Place in the freezer overnight. Roll out the 225 g butter on greaseproof paper to half the size of the dough sheet and freeze.

A good croissant should be light and flaky with a moderately open grain and texture. This is achieved with proper lamination of the dough and butter. The proving temperature should never be too high as the butter will melt prior to baking. This will result in a product that is dense and bread-like while lacking the taste of butter. To obtain a good croissant shape, keep the triangular dough piece tight during the rolling process.

- Remove the dough and butter from the freezer and leave for 10 minutes until both are pliable. Place the butter sheet in the centre of the dough sheet and fold both edges to the centre to obtain 1 layer of butter in the middle. This is known as the French Method.

- Immediately roll out the dough (opened ends) and make a book-fold by folding both sides to the centre and then folding into 2 again to create 4 layers of butter in the dough. Thin down the dough slightly and quickly return the dough to the freezer for ½–1 hour until the dough is firm but not hard.

- Roll out the dough again (opened ends) and fold into 3 to obtain 12 layers of butter. Rest dough in the freezer for ½–1 hour until dough is firm.

- Roll out the dough to about 4 mm thickness and cut into triangles 13 cm by 26 cm. Make a 1-cm slit at the centre of the base of the triangle. With both hands pointed slightly outwards, roll up the dough piece from the wide end. Form a crescent shape.

- Prove dough in a moderately warm place for 1–1½ hours. When dough has doubled in size, brush with egg and bake in a preheated oven at 230°C for 18–20 minutes. Remove croissants immediately and place on a cooling rack.

Danish

Ingredients:

Plain flour (all-purpose flour)	100 g
Strong white flour (bread flour)	400 g
Milk powder	25 g
Bread improver	8 g
Instant dry yeast	10 g
Sugar	50 g
Salt	10 g
Eggs	125 g (2, medium)
Cold water	140 g
Butter	40 g, softened
Butter	225 g, firm

Method:

- With an electric mixer and dough hook at low speed, blend the ingredients (except firm butter) for 6 minutes. Round up the dough and allow it to relax on a flour-dusted work surface for 20 minutes. Roll out the dough to a rectangular shape (length twice the breadth) 1-cm thick.

- Transfer the dough onto a tray and wrap with a plastic sheet. Place in the freezer overnight. Roll out the firm butter on greaseproof paper to half the size of the dough sheet and refrigerate.

- Remove the dough and butter from the refrigerator and leave for 10 minutes until both are pliable. Place the butter sheet in the centre of the dough and fold both edges to the centre to obtain 1 layer of butter in the middle. This is known as the French Method.

Apricot glaze gives the Danish a good shine, making it very appetizing. The glaze can be prepared by boiling agar-agar powder, sugar, glucose syrup and water. The glaze, however, softens the Danish, making it less flaky.

- Immediately roll out the dough and make a book-fold (refer to Croissant recipe).

- Roll out the dough again and fold into 3. Thin down dough slightly and quickly return it to the freezer for ½–1 hour until dough is firm but not hard. Roll out the dough to about 4 mm thick and cut into 12-cm squares. The dough is now ready to be cut into various shapes.

- To make bear paws, place a hot dog across the centre of the dough piece. Wet one edge of the dough with water, fold over and secure it. Using a dough cutter, make 4 cuts and bend the dough piece until an arc shape is formed.

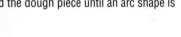

From top: Croissant, Danish.

- To make fresh fruit danish, fold dough over to form a triangle. Using a dough cutter, make 2 cuts 1 cm from the two edges and 10 cm in length. The two cuts must have a gap of 1 cm. Unfold the dough piece and wet the edges. Take the cut sides to the opposite end. They will overlap. Press down to secure and prick holes in the centre with a fork.

- Prove dough in a moderately warm place for 1–1½ hours. When dough has risen doubled in size, brush with egg and bake in a preheated oven at 230°C for 18–20 minutes. Pipe custard on the fruit Danish and top with peaches, strawberries and kiwi fruit. Brush with apricot glaze.

Egg Bagels

Ingredients:

Strong white flour (bread flour)	500 g
Milk powder	10 g
Bread improver	8 g
Instant dry yeast	10 g
Sugar	35 g
Salt	10 g
Egg	40 g (1, small)
Water	280 g
Butter	50 g, softened

Topping

Poppy seeds
Sesame seeds
Multigrain
Semolina

Method:

- With an electric mixer and a dough hook, mix all the dry ingredients for 1 minute on low speed. Add egg and water and continue mixing on low speed for another minute. Change to medium speed for 3 minutes and add butter. Continue mixing for 10 minutes until dough is fully developed.

- Round up dough and place into an airtight container to rise in a warm place for 1 hour until dough is double in bulk. Divide the dough into 100 g pieces. Round up the dough pieces and allow them to rest for 10 minutes.

- Roll each dough piece into an even strip long enough to go completely around the palm of your hand. Overlap the ends of the strips about 2 cm and seal the edges together by rolling forward and backward with the palm of your hand.

- Prove the dough in a warm place for about 30–40 minutes. Brush with egg and sprinkle with poppy seeds, sesame seeds, multigrain or semolina if desired. Bake in a preheated oven at 200°C for 15–20 minutes.

If a chewy bagel is desired, take the bagels when it is halfway through proving and boil in a 5 percent sugar solution for 1 minute before baking. The bagels will also have a shiny appearance due to the syrup treatment.

Mexico Bun

Ingredients:
Sponge

Strong flour (bread flour)	280 g
Instant dry yeast	3 g
Water	170 g

Dough

Strong flour (bread flour)	120 g
Milk powder	15 g
Bread improver	6 g
Instant dry yeast	8 g
Sugar	80 g
Salt	6 g
Egg	50 g (1, medium)
Egg yolk	20 g, (1, medium)
Butter	60 g
Butter, firm, for filling	

Method:

- With an electric mixer and dough hook, prepare the sponge by mixing the three ingredients on low speed for 3 minutes. The sponge should be firm, dry and cool (24°C) to the touch. Leave the sponge for 4–5 hours in an airtight container at about 27°C.

- When the sponge is ready, prepare the dough. Place the remaining dry ingredients into the mixer and add egg, egg yolk and water. Mix on low speed. Immediately cut sponge into a few pieces and add to the mixture over 1 minute.

- Increase speed to medium and mix for 2 minutes. Add butter and mix for another 7–10 minutes until dough is fully developed. Round up the dough and rest it for 10 minutes. Divide the dough into 55 g pieces and round up again.

- After another 10 minutes, flatten dough with the palm of your hand and wrap a piece of firm butter (10 g) inside.

- Prove dough for 45 minutes in a warm place until the dough is almost double in size. Pipe the Mexico bun topping (see recipe) in a continuous concentric circle, starting from the center, over the top of the bun until the surface is fully covered. Sprinkle chocolate chips over it.

- Bake in a preheated oven at 200°C for 12–15 minutes until the buns turn slightly brown.

The addition of the extra egg yolk to the dough results in a softer eating bun with a nice golden crumb colour. This is due to the presence of lecithin in egg yolk, an emulsifier and a bread softener, which helps to keep the bread from becoming stale too soon. Egg yolk can be added into most breads at 5–10 percent of the flour weight.

From left: Mexico Bun, Egg Bagels.

Mexico Bun Topping

Ingredients:

Butter	190 g
Sugar	190 g
Eggs	190 g (3, large)
Plain flour (all purpose flour)	200 g
Vanilla flavouring	9 g

Method:

- With a paddle, blend butter and sugar on medium speed for 3 minutes until fluffy. Add egg slowly and continue mixing on medium speed for another 3 minutes. Fold in flour and vanilla flavouring on low speed until well blended.

- Leave the batter in the refrigerator until the buns are fully proved. Pipe approximately 45 g of topping over the each proved bun.

Crumpets

Ingredients:

Superfine flour (high ratio cake flour)	300 g
Lukewarm water (37°C)	375 g
Sugar	2 g
Salt	5 g
Instant dry yeast	6 g
Baking powder	12 g

Method:

- With an electric mixer, whisk flour, lukewarm water (280 g), sugar and salt on medium speed for 3 minutes. Put yeast in the remaining water (95 g) and add to the batter. Mix on high speed for 2 minutes.

- Ferment the batter in a bowl wrapped with cling film. Let it stand in a warm place for 30–45 minutes until the batter rises and then falls.

- Add baking powder and whisk on medium speed for 1 minute. Ferment the batter by placing in a warm place for 30 minutes.

- Heat a clean griddle or frying pan over moderately low heat for about 3 minutes until very hot. Put several well-greased crumpet rings on the griddle and pour batter to two-third the height of the rings.

- After 2–3 minutes, the top surface will start to set and will be covered with holes. Remove the ring with tongs and flip the crumpets over with a spatula. Cook the crumpet for another 2–3 minutes or until golden brown.

As soon as the batter is poured into the ring, holes should begin to form within 2 minutes. If holes do not form, whisk the remaining batter in a little lukewarm water. If the batter is too thin and runs out of the ring, gently fold in a little flour into the remaining batter.

English Muffin

Ingredients:

Strong white flour (bread flour)	500 g
Bread improver	8 g
Baking powder	5 g
Instant dry yeast	15 g
Salt	8 g
Dry wheat gluten	5 g
Calcium propionate	3 g
Honey	15 g
Butter	15 g
Cold water	460 g
Semolina	for coating

Method:

- With an electric mixer and dough hook, blend all the ingredients and 400 g of the cold water on low speed for 1 minute and then medium speed for 10 minutes. Add the rest of the water (60 g) and mix for another 5 minutes until dough is fully developed. The dough is slack and slightly soft.

- Ferment the dough for 1 hour and divide into 55 g pieces. Mould the pieces round and rest them for 10 minutes. Coat the dough pieces with semolina and flatten with a rolling pin. Place them in oil-coated rings 8-cm wide and 2.5-cm thick on greased baking trays.

- Prove for 45 minutes In a warm place until the dough reaches the top of the rings. Place another baking tray over the rings and bake in a preheated oven for 15–20 minutes at 200°C until the tops turn golden brown.

To make wholemeal muffins, replace 50 g of flour with wheat bran and add another 15 g water to the recipe. By placing a heavy tray over the muffin rings, a flat and round muffin will be produced.

Clockwise from top right: Crumpets, English Muffin.

Butter Roll

Ingredients:

Strong white flour (bread flour)	500 g
Milk powder	15 g
Bread improver	8 g
Instant dry yeast	10 g
Sugar	75 g
Salt	8 g
Egg	75g (1½, small)
Cold water	250 g
Butter	75 g, softened

Method:

- With an electric mixer and dough hook at low speed, mix all the dry ingredients together for 1 minute. Add eggs and water, and continue mixing on low speed for another minute. Change to medium speed and mix for 5 minutes until dough is half developed. Carefully add softened butter a little at a time and mix for another 7–10 minutes on medium speed until dough is fully developed.

- Transfer the dough onto a flour-dusted work surface and round up dough with both hands. Place dough into an airtight container and let it rise in a warm place for 1 hour until dough doubles in bulk. Divide dough into 100 g portions. Use cupped hands to mould the dough into smooth round balls.

- After 15 minutes, roll out the dough and mould with your fingers into strips about 30-cm long. Twist the strips into double knots and figure-8 rolls. Place the rolls 5 cm apart on a greased tray and prove in a warm place for 1 hour until dough doubles in size.

- Brush the tops with egg glaze and bake in a preheated oven at 200°C for 15 minutes or until golden brown. Remove and cool on a wire rack.

It is necessary to dust a little flour on the table when rolling out the dough to prevent sticking. Avoid using too much dusting flour as this will dry up the dough. For the butter rolls to turn out nicely, it is important that each strip is of even thickness throughout and that they are tightly rolled when twisting into shape.

Pandan Coconut Heart

Ingredients:

Strong white flour (bread flour)	500 g
Bread improver	8 g
Instant dry yeast	14 g
Sugar	110 g
Salt	5 g
Coconut cream powder	25 g
Egg	70 g (1, large)
Pandan leaf water	225 g
Pandan flavouring	10 g
Shortening	40 g

Method:

- With an electric mixer and a dough hook at low speed, blend all the dry ingredients together for 1 minute. Add egg, pandan leaf water and pandan flavouring and continue mixing on low speed for another minute. Change to medium speed and mix for 3 minutes.

- Add shortening in 2 portions and mix for 7–10 minutes on medium speed until dough is fully developed. Transfer the dough onto a flour-dusted work surface and round it up with both hands. Leave in an airtight container for 1 hour until the dough is double in bulk.

- Divide the dough into 55 g pieces and mould round. Rest the dough for 10 minutes and remould into balls. Let the dough rest for another 10 minutes. Press the dough down with the palm of your hand. Fill with 30 g of coconut filling (*see recipe*). With your thumb and forefinger, pleat around the dough to seal the filling inside the bun.

- Rest the filled dough pieces for another 2 minutes and flatten into an oval shape with a rolling pin. Fold into half lengthwise to form an elongated semi-circle, then fold in half again. The dough piece should look like a quarter semi-circle. Make a cut at centre of the folded dough piece. The cut should be three-quarter way up the dough piece. Turn up to expose the cut ends, moulding it into a heart shape with your hands.

- Place the buns on a greased baking tray and prove for 40–50 minutes in a warm place. Brush egg wash on the top of the buns and bake in a preheated oven at 190°C for 12–15 minutes until glossy and golden brown. Turn out and cool on a wire rack.

This recipe has a high sugar content. Watch that the baking temperature does not exceed 190°C or the buns will burn. Do not apply too much dusting flour on the dough when putting in the filling. The flour will prevent the bottom of the dough from forming a good seam, allowing the filling to ooze out during baking.

From front: Pandan Coconut Heart, Butter Roll.

Coconut Filling

Ingredients:

Coconut	400 g, freshly grated
Sugar	180 g
Egg	60 g (1, medium)
Butter	65 g
Treacle	20 g

Method:

- Cook the grated coconut with butter, treacle and sugar on a low flame for 10 minutes. Cool and add egg.

Swiss Buns and Fingers

Ingredients:

Strong white flour (bread flour)	500 g
Milk powder	15 g
Bread improver	8 g
Instant dry yeast	12 g
Sugar	60 g
Salt	8 g
Cold water	300 g
Shortening	60 g

Piping

Fruit jam
Fresh cream

Method:

- With an electric mixer and dough hook at low speed, blend the dry ingredients together for about 1 minute. Add water and continue mixing on low speed for another minute. Put in shortening and mix on medium speed for 12 minutes until the dough is fully developed.

- Transfer the dough onto a flour-dusted work surface and round up the dough. Place the dough into an airtight container and let it rise in a warm place for 1 hour until the dough is double in bulk.

- Divide into 75 g pieces and mould round. Rest the dough pieces for 10 minutes. Remould the dough pieces round to make buns and shape them long for fingers. Prove the dough in a warm, draught-free place for 1 hour.

- Bake in a preheated oven at 225°C for 10–12 minutes. After baking, transfer onto a cooling wire. When cool, split the buns and fingers and decorate with jam and fresh cream.

 Fresh strawberries, kiwi fruit and canned peaches can be sliced thinly and added to the buns and fingers for greater taste and appeal.

Brioche

Ingredients:

Strong white flour (bread flour)	400 g
Bread improver	6 g
Instant dry yeast	11 g
Sugar	60 g
Salt	6 g
Milk powder	8 g
Eggs	200 g (4, small)
Cold water	70 g
Butter	140 g, softened

Method:

- With an electric mixer and a dough hook at low speed, blend the dry ingredients together for 1 minute. Add eggs then water and continue mixing on low speed for another minute. Change to medium speed and mix for 5 minutes until dough is half developed.

- Add softened butter a little at a time and mix for 7–10 minutes on medium speed until dough is fully developed.

- Transfer the dough onto a flour-dusted work surface and round up dough with both hands. Place dough into an airtight container and let it rise in a warm place for 1 hour until dough doubles in bulk.

- Divide the dough into 14 pieces at 60 g each and another 14 pieces at 10 g each. Mould the pieces into smooth round balls. Leave for 10 minutes. Round up the dough balls and transfer the large balls into brioche moulds. Use your forefingers to make an indentation in the centre of the large ball and immediately place the small ball on top. Finish up by pressing the small ball down into the larger ball with your finger to secure the pieces together. Prove in a warm place for 1 hour until the dough is double in bulk.

- Brush the tops with egg glaze. Place the moulds on a baking tray and bake in a preheated oven at 190°C for 15–20 minutes until glossy and golden. Turn out and cool on a wire rack.

 Chef's Tip: Rounding up the dough pieces twice, prior to placing them in the brioche moulds, will produce bread with better volume and texture.

Kaiser Roll

Ingredients:
Sponge

Strong white flour (bread flour)	350 g
Instant dry yeast	4 g
Water	210 g

Dough

Strong white flour (bread flour)	150 g
Bread improver	8 g
Instant dry yeast	5 g
Salt	10 g
Water	110 g
Shortening	5 g

Method:

* With an electric mixer and dough hook, prepare the sponge by mixing the 3 ingredients on low speed for 3 minutes. The sponge should be firm, dry and cool (24°C) to the touch. Ferment the sponge for 4–5 hours in an airtight container at about 27°C.

* When the sponge is ready, prepare the dough. Place the remaining dry ingredients into the mixer. Add water and mix on low speed. Immediately cut sponge into a few pieces and add to the mixture over 1 minute. Increase to medium speed and mix for 2 minutes. Add shortening and mix for another 5–7 minutes until the dough is fully developed.

* Round up and rest the dough for 10 minutes. Divide the dough into 60 g pieces and mould round. Leave the dough to rest for 10 minutes. Remould the dough pieces into balls and place onto a lightly greased tray. Rest the dough pieces for 15 minutes and then stamp with a special kaiser roll cutter. Wet the surface and coat with sesame or poppy seeds.

* Prove in a warm place for 40–50 minutes until dough is double in bulk. Preheat the oven to 230°C. Bake with a tray of water to generate steam for 12–15 minutes until the bread turns golden brown.

Proving of this dough is best carried out at 32°C. The humidity must not be too high (75 percent relative humidity).

Lemon Buns

Ingredients:

Strong flour (bread flour)	400 g
Milk powder	15 g
Bread improver	6 g
Instant dry yeast	12 g
Sugar	80 g
Salt	6 g
Egg	50 g (1, medium)
Water	20 g
Butter	60 g, softened
Butter, firm, for filling	

Method:

* With an electric mixer and dough hook at slow speed, mix the dry ingredients together for 1 minute. Add egg and water and continue to mix on slow speed for another minute. Change to medium speed and mix for 4–5 minutes until dough is half developed. Add softened butter in a few stages and mix for 7–10 minutes on medium speed until dough is fully developed.

* Round up the dough and rest it for 10 minutes. Divide into 55 g pieces and round up again. Leave for 10 minutes. Then flatten dough pieces with the palm of your hand and wrap a piece of firm butter (10 g) inside. Top with 35 g of lemon topping (*see recipe*) and mould the dough into an oval shape.

* Rest the dough for 15 minutes and mark the surface of the buns with a scrapper to form diamond-shaped motifs. Prove the dough for 50 minutes in a warm and dry place until the dough is double in bulk.

* Bake in a preheated oven at 190°C for 12–15 minutes until the buns are golden brown at the base but not the surface.

Do not leave the dough to prove in an area with high humidity as the topping will soften and the markings on the buns will disappear. Watch the buns as they bake and try not to over-bake them, as the buns will discolour, making it less attractive. After baking, the topping should be firm and taste like cookie dough.

From front: Lemon Buns, Kaiser Roll.

Lemon Bun Topping

Ingredients:

Butter	75 g
Sugar	180 g
Emulsifier	6 g
Eggs	85 g (2, small)
Plain flour (all purpose flour)	270 g
Milk powder	15 g
Baking powder	3 g
Coloured lemon flavouring	6 g

Method:

• With a paddle, blend butter, sugar and emulsifier on medium speed for 3 minutes until fluffy. Add eggs and flavouring and mix for another 3 minutes.

• Fold in flour and milk powder on slow speed until well blended. Use the topping immediately as it will start to dry up.

Chicken Frankfurter Roll

Ingredients:

Sponge

Strong flour (bread flour)	280 g
Instant dry yeast	3 g
Water	170 g

Dough

Strong flour (bread flour)	120 g
Milk powder	15 g
Bread improver	6 g
Instant dry yeast	8 g
Sugar	80 g
Salt	6 g
Egg	50 g (1, medium)
Water	20 g
Butter	60 g, softened

Filling

Chicken frankfurters	14

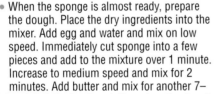

Method:

- With an electric mixer and dough hook, prepare the sponge by mixing the 3 ingredients on low speed for 3 minutes. The sponge should be firm, dry and cool (24°C) to the touch. Leave to rise for 4–5 hours in an airtight container at about 27°C.

- When the sponge is almost ready, prepare the dough. Place the dry ingredients into the mixer. Add egg and water and mix on low speed. Immediately cut sponge into a few pieces and add to the mixture over 1 minute. Increase to medium speed and mix for 2 minutes. Add butter and mix for another 7–10 minutes until dough is fully developed. Round up the dough and let it rest for 10 minutes. Divide the dough into 55 g pieces and round up again.

- Leave the dough pieces to rest for 5–10 minutes and then roll out each dough piece with a rolling pin to a length of 35 cm with the ends tapering. Take a dough strip and wrap it around a frankfurter by forming 5–6 coils of dough over it. Prove rolls for 1 hour in a warm place until the dough doubles in size

- Brush egg over the surface of the rolls and bake in a preheated oven at 200°C for 12–15 minutes until the rolls turn golden brown.

Chef's Tip: This is a sweet bun dough and is ideal with sweet or savoury filling. The sponge should just be blended together and not over mixed, as the 4 hours of proving will help to restructure the gluten, maturing the dough in the process.

Hamburger Bun

Ingredients:

Sponge

Strong white flour (bread flour)	350 g
Instant dry yeast	4 g
Water	210 g

Dough

Strong white flour (bread flour)	150 g
Milk powder	10 g
Bread improver	8 g
Instant dry yeast	5 g
Sugar	50 g
Salt	10 g
Water	90 g
Shortening	50 g

Method:

- With an electric mixer and dough hook, prepare the sponge by mixing the 3 ingredients on low speed for 3 minutes. The sponge should be firm, dry and cool (24°C) to the touch. Ferment the sponge for 4–5 hours in an airtight container at about 27°C.

- When the sponge is ready, prepare the dough. Place the remaining dry ingredients into the mixer. Add water and mix on low speed. Immediately cut sponge into a few pieces and add to the mixture over 1 minute. Increase to medium speed and mix for 2 minutes. Add shortening and mix for another 5–7 minutes until dough is fully developed.

- Round up and rest the dough for 10 minutes. Divide the dough into 70 g pieces and round up. After another 10 minutes, round up the dough pieces again and flatten slightly with the palm of your hand.

- Prove in a warm place for 40–50 minutes until the dough doubles in size. Brush with egg and bake in a preheated oven at 220°C for 12–15 minutes until the bread turns golden brown.

Chef's Tip: The amount of yeast added in the dough stage can be reduced or omitted if desired. The proving time, however, will need to be increased proportionally. Slack or soft dough is ideal for making hamburger buns.

From left: Chicken Frankfurter Roll, Hamburger Bun.

Butter Top Bread

Ingredients:

Sponge

Strong white flour (bread flour)	350 g
Instant dry yeast	4 g
Water	210 g

Dough

Strong white flour (bread flour)	150 g
Milk powder	10 g
Bread improver	8 g
Instant dry yeast	5 g
Sugar	50 g
Salt	10 g
Water	90 g
Butter	50 g, softened

Method:

- With an electric mixer and dough hook, prepare the sponge by mixing the 3 ingredients on low speed for 3 minutes. The sponge should be firm, dry and cool (24°C) to the touch. Leave the sponge to rise for 4–5 hours in an airtight container at around 27°C.

- When the sponge has risen, prepare the dough. Place the dry ingredients into the mixer. Add water and mix on low speed. Immediately cut the sponge into a few pieces and add to the mixture over 1 minute. Increase to medium speed and mix for 2 minutes. Add butter and mix for another 5–7 minutes until dough is fully developed.

- Round up and rest the dough for 10 minutes. Divide the dough into 300 g portions and mould round. Rest dough for 10 minutes. Roll out the dough pieces and mould each piece into a cylindrical shape to fit the tin. Prove in a warm place for 1 hour until the dough doubles in bulk.

- With a sharp blade, make a cut along the centre of the loaf and pipe softened butter on it. Bake at 200°C for 25 minutes until the bread turns golden brown.

Chef's Tip: It is best to cut the loaf when it is three quarters through proving so that the dough will not collapse. Butter should be pliable and not melted when applied on the top.

Pita Bread

Ingredients:

Sponge

Strong white flour (bread flour)	350 g
Instant dry yeast	4 g
Water	210 g

Dough

Strong white flour (bread flour)	150 g
Malt flour	5 g
Milk powder	10 g
Bread improver	8 g
Instant dry yeast	5 g
Sugar	35 g
Salt	10 g
Water	100 g
Shortening	35 g

Method

- With an electric mixer and dough hook, prepare the sponge by mixing the 3 ingredients on low speed for 3 minutes. The sponge should be firm, dry and cool (24°C) to the touch. Ferment the sponge for 4–5 hours in an airtight container at about 27°C.

- When the sponge is ready, prepare the dough. Place the remaining dry ingredients into the mixer. Add water and mix on low speed. Immediately cut sponge into a few pieces and add to the mixture over 1 minute. Increase to medium speed and mix for 2 minutes. Add shortening and mix for another 5–7 minutes until dough is fully developed.

- Round up and rest the dough for 10 minutes. Divide the dough into 90 g pieces and mould round. Rest dough for 10 minutes. Pin out each dough piece into a round shape about 2-mm thick. Prove in a warm place for 30–40 minutes until the dough is double in bulk.

- Bake in a preheated oven at 250°C for 5–6 minutes until golden brown. Slice in half, fill with desired filling and serve.

Chef's Tip: Baking is best carried out on the hearth of the oven without the use of baking trays. A high oven temperature is necessary for the dough to puff up during the first few minutes of baking.

From front: Pita Bread, Butter Top Bread.

Foccacia Bread

Ingredients:

Strong white flour (bread flour)	500 g
Malt flour (optional)	10 g
Bread improver	8 g
Instant dry yeast	10 g
Oregano	3 g
Rosemary	3 g, plus extra for topping
Ground black pepper	1 g
Salt	8 g
Cold water	310 g
Olive oil	30 g

Method:

- With an electric mixer and dough hook at low speed, blend the dry ingredients together for 1 minute. Add water and mix on low speed for 2 minutes. Add olive oil and continue to mix for 12–15 minutes on medium speed until dough is fully developed. The dough should be slightly slack at this stage.

- Place dough into an airtight container coated with olive oil and leave to rise in a warm place for 1 hour. Then gently press out the air from the dough and let it to rest for 5 minutes. Prepare a baking tray by applying olive oil over it.

All breads must be transferred onto a wire rack to cool as soon as it is removed from the oven. This will prevent condensation which makes the base of the bread soggy. Ideally, all breads must be cooled to an internal temperature of 35°C before it is wrapped in plastic bags. This will prevent condensation and mould growth.

- Pin out the dough to fill the baking tray evenly. Prove for 1 hour in a warm place until dough is double in bulk. Make deep holes all over the surface of the dough with your fingers. Brush the top with olive oil and sprinkle some rosemary over it.

- With your fingertips, poke the dough all over to make deep dimples. Bake for 20 minutes in a preheated oven at 220°C until crisp-crusted underneath and lightly brown on top. Immediately, brush olive oil over the bread. Transfer the bread onto a wire rack to cool.

Ciabatta

Ingredients:

Strong white flour (bread flour)	500 g
Malt flour	10 g
Bread improver	8 g
Instant dry yeast	5 g
Salt	10 g
Cold water	360 g
Olive oil	10 g

Method:

- With an electric mixer and dough hook at low speed, blend the dry ingredients together for 1 minute. Add water and continue mixing on low speed for 2 minutes. Add olive oil and mix on medium speed for 12–15 minutes until the dough is fully developed.

- Transfer the dough onto a flour-dusted work surface and round up dough with both hands. Place the dough into an oiled plastic container. Leave it to rise in a warm place for 1½ hours until dough is double in bulk.

- Remove and place the dough on a flour-dusted work surface. Divide into 3 pieces of 300 g each. Dust the dough pieces with flour and gently stretch them lengthwise before placing on a silicon paper-lined tray. Prove in a warm, humid and draught-free place for 20 minutes.

- Preheat the oven to 230°C. Bake with a tray of water to generate steam for the first 10 minutes of baking time. Open the door of the oven and remove any water remaining. Reduce the temperature to 210°C and bake for another 15 minutes. After baking, transfer onto a cooling rack.

 The dough must be handled carefully during scaling (after proving) to ensure that the open crumb structure and shape, that is characteristic of ciabatta, is maintained.

From front: Foccacia Bread, Ciabata.

Roti Canai

Ingredients:

Plain flour (all- purpose flour)	500 g
Sugar	25 g
Salt	3 g
Water	275 g
Milk	50 g
Egg	50 g (1, small)
Butter	15 g, softened

Method:

- Premix the dry ingredients on low speed for 1 minute. Add the rest of the ingredients and continue to mix on medium speed for 12–15 minutes until the dough is fully developed. The dough must be slack or soft.

- Leave dough for 10 minutes and divide into 90 g pieces. Round up the dough into balls, rub butter all over and let the dough rest in the refrigerator in a greased container for at least 3 hours.

- Work the dough into a translucent sheet. Apply cooking oil on the work surface and hands and press down on the dough to flatten it. Continue by flattening and pushing out the dough in all directions until the dough starts to spring back. Hold the dough with both hands and gently stretch and flip the dough until it is very thin.

- Sprinkle some oil over the stretched dough and fold the four sides to the centre to create a square. Leave for 10 minutes. Preheat a hot plate or frying pan and apply oil all over it. With both your hands, pull and stretch the dough slightly before transferring onto the hot plate.

- Cook on the hot plate for 30 seconds. Flip the roti canai over and cook the other side for another 30 seconds. The cooked roti canai should be crisp, speckled with brown patches and slightly puffy.

Chapati

Ingredients:

Plain flour (all-purpose flour)	75 g
Fine wholemeal flour (atta flour)	225 g
Salt	5 g
Cold water	200 g

Method:

- With an electric mixer and dough hook at low speed, blend the dry ingredients together for 1 minute. Add water and mix on low speed for 6–8 minutes until dough is smooth.

- Transfer the dough onto a flour-dusted work surface and round up. Place dough into an airtight container and let it rest for 20 minutes.

- Divide the dough into 55 g pieces. Round up and leave for 10 minutes. Lightly coat flour around the dough pieces. Press down and roll each dough piece out with a rolling pin into a circle about 18-cm wide and 3-mm thick.

- Heat a large cast-iron frying pan or a heavy griddle until hot. Cook the chapati for about 30 seconds until the top surface begins to change colour. With a spatula, flip the chapati over so that the cooked surface is on top. Cook for another 30 seconds. Quickly flip it over again and the dough will start to puff up in the centre.

- Using a dry dishtowel, press down on the centre so that the steam from the centre will be forced out to the edges causing it to cook evenly. Flip the chapati over again and repeat with the other side until both sides are properly cooked.

- Place on a clean dishtowel and lightly brush the top with ghee or melted butter. Cover with another towel to keep warm.

This recipe uses plain (all-purpose) flour as it has lower protein content (9–10 percent) as compared to bread flour (12–13 percent). Flours with high protein content will cause the dough to be too elastic and difficult to stretch. A longer rest time, preferably overnight, in the refrigerator will assist the dough to relax, making it easier to stretch into a thin film. Avoid making the dough too stiff, as it will be impossible to stretch thinly. This will result in a thick mass that is difficult to cook and will be unpalatable.

If atta flour is not available, you can use wholemeal flour by sieving it to remove the coarser bits of bran. In this case use 300 g of the sieved wholemeal flour without the addition of plain flour.

From left: Chapati, Roti Canai.

Waffle

Ingredients:

Ferment

Plain flour (all-purpose flour)	55 g
Instant dry yeast	3 g
Water	160 g, warmed to 37°C

Dough

Plain flour (all-purpose flour)	245 g
Milk powder	10 g
Baking powder	9 g
Sugar	12 g
Salt	3 g
Eggs	160 g (3, small)
Vanilla flavouring	6 g
Emulsifier	8 g
Water	120 g
Dairy whipping cream	65 g

Method:

- With a hand whisk, prepare the ferment by mixing the 3 ingredients together. Ferment the mixture for 30–45 minutes in a container at about 27°C. The ferment will rise and then fall.

- To prepare the dough, premix the dry ingredients and set aside.

- In another bowl, whisk eggs, flavouring and emulsifier on high speed for 3 minutes. Add the ferment and continue to whisk on medium speed for 2 minutes. Add the premixed dry ingredients then water in 3 portions and mix on medium speed for 2 minutes.

- Sieve batter to remove any lumps. Leave batter for 20–30 minutes before using.

- Preheat a waffle iron to 200°C and pour the batter evenly over the iron. Cover and allow to cook for 2–3 minutes. The waffle is ready when it is golden brown.

This recipe produces a crispy waffle with an excellent flavour. It can however be further enhanced by adding 10 g of malt flour. The waffle mixture can be prepared a day ahead and kept in the refrigerator for use the next day.

Honey Pretzel

Ingredients:

Sponge

Strong flour (bread flour)	250 g
Instant dry yeast	4 g
Water	150 g

Dough

Plain flour (all-purpose flour)	250 g
Baking powder	3 g
Bread improver	8 g
Instant dry yeast	10 g
Salt	8 g
Honey	150 g
Egg	25 g (½, small)
Water	40 g
Alkaline water	3 g
(Sodium silicate and soda ash mixture)	
Butter	150 g, softened

Method:

- With an electric mixer and dough hook, prepare the sponge by mixing the 3 ingredients on low speed for 3 minutes. The sponge should be firm, dry and cool (24°C) to the touch. Ferment the sponge for 4–5 hours in an airtight container at about 27°C. The sponge can also be fermented overnight in the fridge.

- When the sponge is ready, prepare the dough. Place the remaining dry ingredients into the mixer. Add honey, egg, water and alkaline water. Start mixing on low speed and add the sponge over 1 minute. Increase to medium speed and mix for 2 minutes. Add butter a little at a time and mix for another 7–10 minutes until the dough is fully developed. Round up and rest the dough for 20 minutes.

- Cut the dough into 100 g pieces and mould into 75-cm long strips. To make a pretzel shape, cross the ends of a strip to make a loop. Twist the crossed ends once and fold across the loop.

- Prove the pretzels for 1 hour until doubled in size. Brush egg glaze over the pretzels and sprinkle multigrain or seeds of your choice over them. Bake in a preheated oven at 180°C for 12–15 minutes until golden brown. Cool on a wire rack.

 Adding alkaline water to the dough causes the gluten in the dough to be more pliable. This makes the job of rolling and moulding the dough much easier. Alkali imparts a darker colour to the crust of the pretzel.

From left: Honey Pretzel, Waffle.

Mini Chinese Doughnut

Ingredients:

Plain flour (all-purpose flour)	500 g
Baking powder	55 g
Instant dry yeast	2 g
Sugar	13 g
Salt	7 g
Ammonium bicarbonate	5 g
Water	370 g

Method:

- Sieve flour and baking powder twice. Fold in yeast and put into the mixing bowl.

- Dissolve sugar, salt and ammonium bicarbonate in water and pour into the flour mixture. Mix for 1–2 minutes on low speed until dough is formed. Leave the dough to rest for 20–30 minutes in the mixing bowl. Cover to prevent a skin from forming.

- With a plastic scrapper dipped in oil, scrape around the sides of the bowl and push the dough underneath so as to stretch and tighten the dough and remove any gas bubbles. Rest the dough for another 20–30 minutes and repeat the above process. The dough is now smoother and can be rested in the refrigerator for a minimum of 2 hours.

- Dust flour on the work surface and cut dough into 2 pieces. Stretch each dough piece until it is about 6.5-cm wide and 1.5-cm thick. Rest the dough for 15 minutes and cut into 2.5-cm wide strips.

- Wet the centre of a strip lengthwise with a stick dipped in water. Place another strip on top. With your hands on each end of the dough strips, stretch by pulling the dough with your thumb and forefinger until it is 10 cm long.

- Preheat some cooking oil to 180°C and place the stretched dough gently into it. Once the dough floats to the surface, use a pair of chopsticks to turn the dough over continuously to allow the dough to expand evenly. Fry for 2–3 minutes until the doughnut is golden brown in colour.

Chef's Tip: When stretching the dough, it is best to hold the dough 1 cm from the ends. This way, the ends of the two pieces of dough will not stick together and will be allowed to expand fully.

Doughnut

Ingredients:
Sponge

Strong flour (bread flour)	350 g
Instant dry yeast	4 g
Water	210 g

Dough

Strong flour (bread flour)	50 g
Plain flour (all purpose flour)	100 g
Milk powder	30 g
Baking powder	10 g
Bread improver	8 g
Instant dry yeast	8 g
Sugar	75 g
Salt	5 g
Egg	30 g, or ½, medium
Water	40 g
Butter	60 g, softened

Method:

- With an electric mixer and dough hook, prepare the sponge by mixing the 3 ingredients on low speed for 3 minutes. The sponge should be firm, dry and cool (24°C) to the touch. Ferment the sponge for 4–5 hours in an airtight container at about 27°C.

- When the sponge is fermented, prepare the dough. Place the remaining dry ingredients into the mixer. Add egg and water and mix on slow speed. Immediately cut sponge into a few pieces and add to the mixture over 1 minute. Increase speed to medium and mix for 2 minutes. Add butter and mix for another 7–10 minutes until dough is fully developed.

- Round up the dough and rest on a flour-dusted work surface for 15 minutes. Roll out the dough slightly and shrink the dough, making sure it does not stick to the table. With a doughnut cutter, press down firmly on the dough and twist so that the doughnuts can be easily released.

- Prove dough for 45 minutes in a warm place until the dough doubles in size. Fry in hot oil (180°C) for 45 seconds on each side until golden brown.

Chef's Tip: It is important to maintain the frying temperature at 180°C. A lower frying temperature will take longer to cook, resulting in oily doughnuts. Too high a temperature will cause the oil to smoke and also result in burnt and half cooked doughnuts.

From left: Mini Chinese Doughnut, Doughnut.

Cream Cheese Raisin Bread

Ingredients:

Cream cheese	400 g
Sugar	60 g
Strong white flour (bread flour)	500 g
Bread improver	8 g
Dry wheat gluten	10 g
Instant dry yeast	13 g
Salt	8 g
Eggs	125 g (2, large)
Cold water	100 g
Raisins	200 g

Topping
Walnuts
Cream Cheese
Poppy seeds

Method:

- With an electric mixer and paddle on medium speed, mix cream cheese and sugar for 2 minutes until softened. Remove the mixture and attach a dough hook.

- Mix all the dry ingredients together for 1 minute on slow speed. Add eggs then water and continue mixing on slow speed for another minute. Change to medium speed and mix for 5 minutes, and then add the cream cheese mixture. Continue to mix for another 7–10 minutes until dough is fully developed. Mix in raisins on low speed over 1 minute making sure not to crush the raisins.

Cream cheese should only be added halfway through mixing to allow the gluten to develop. Lemon flavouring can also be added to enhance the taste of the bread.

- Transfer the dough onto a flour-dusted work surface and round up dough with both hands. Place dough into an airtight container and let it rise in a warm place for 1 hour until dough is double in bulk.

- Divide the dough into 80 g pieces. Round up and rest the dough pieces for 10 minutes, then remould into balls. Place 4 dough balls together and prove dough for 45–50 minutes in a warm, draught-free room until dough doubles in size.

- Brush beaten egg over the dough. Place a walnut over each bun and pipe softened cream cheese over it. Sprinkle poppy seeds and bake in a preheated oven at 200°C for 15 minutes until the top turns golden brown.

Raisin Teacakes

Ingredients:

Strong white flour (bread flour)	500 g
Milk powder	15 g
Bread improver	8 g
Instant dry yeast	10 g
Sugar	30 g
Salt	10 g
Egg	25 g (½, small)
Cold water	290 g
Shortening	30 g
Raisins	75 g

Method:

- With an electric mixer and dough hook at low speed, blend the dry ingredients together for about 1 minute. Add egg then water and continue mixing on low speed for another minute. Put in shortening and mix on medium speed for 12 minutes until dough is fully developed. Add raisins on low speed and mix for 1 minute.

- Transfer the dough onto a flour-dusted work surface and round up dough with both hands. Place dough into an airtight container and let it rise in a warm place for 1 hour until dough is double in bulk.

- Divide the dough into 90 g pieces and mould round. Rest dough for 10 minutes. Roll out the dough pieces round with a diameter of 8 cm. Prove dough in a warm, draught-free place for 1 hour.

- Brush the top of the dough pieces with egg wash and bake in a preheated oven at 230°C for 10–12 minutes. Cool on a wire rack.

To make mixed fruit teacakes, add 25 g of mixed peel to the recipe.

From left: Cream Cheese Raisin Bread, Raisin Teacakes.

Cinnamon Roll

Ingredients:
Sponge

Strong flour (bread flour)	420 g
Instant dry yeast	4 g
Water	250 g

Dough

Strong flour (bread flour)	30 g
Plain flour (all purpose flour)	150 g
Milk powder	30 g
Bread improver	7 g
Instant dry yeast	12 g
Sugar	120 g
Salt	9 g
Eggs	90 g, (2, small) chilled
Butter	90 g

Filling & Topping

Raisins	200 g
Almond flakes	120 g, plus extra for sprinkling
Brown sugar	60 g
Ground cinnamon	2 g

Method:

- With an electric mixer and dough hook, prepare the sponge by mixing the 3 ingredients on low speed for 3 minutes. The sponge should be firm, dry and cool (24°C) to the touch. Leave the sponge to rise for 4–5 hours in an airtight container at about 27°C.

- When the sponge has risen, prepare the dough. Place the dry ingredients into the mixer. Add cold eggs and begin to mix on low speed. Immediately cut sponge into a few pieces and add to the mixture over 1 minute. Increase speed to medium and mix for 2 minutes. Add butter and mix for another 7–10 minutes. Round up the dough and rest on a flour-dusted table for 15 minutes.

- Roll out the dough into a 1-cm thick sheet, measuring 30 cm by 50 cm. Brush melted butter over the dough and sprinkle with raisins and almond flakes. Premix the brown sugar and ground cinnamon and sprinkle evenly over the raisins and almonds.

- Roll the dough down lengthwise like a Swiss roll and apply water on the seam. Brush melted butter all over the dough. Cut into 12 pieces and place into a 6-cm high tray measuring 30 cm by 40 cm in 3 rows of 4.

- Prove dough for 1 hour in a warm place until the dough doubles in size. Brush the surface of the rolls with beaten egg and sprinkle with almond flakes. Bake in a preheated oven at 190°C for 25–30 minutes until golden brown.

 For easy release of bread, grease the baking tin well. Placing the rolls close to each other prevents them from drying out during baking.

Raisin Bread

Ingredients:

Strong white flour (bread flour)	400 g
Milk powder	16 g
Bread improver	6 g
Instant dry yeast	10 g
Sugar	55 g
Salt	6 g
Egg	25 g (½, small)
Cold water	225 g
Butter	60 g
Raisins	300 g

Method:

- With an electric mixer and dough hook at low speed, blend the dry ingredients together for 1 minute. Add egg then water and continue mixing on low speed for another minute. Increase to medium speed and mix for 5 minutes. Add butter and mix for another 7–10 minutes until the dough is fully developed. Mix in raisins on low speed over 1 minute making sure not to crush the raisins.

- Transfer the dough onto a flour-dusted work surface and round up the dough with both hands. Place the dough into an airtight container and let it rise in a warm place for 1–1½ hours until the dough is double in bulk.

- Divide the dough into 3 pieces, each weighing 350 g. Round up and rest the dough pieces for 15 minutes.

- Press down and roll the dough out with a rolling pin. Mould it firmly with the fingertips into a cylindrical shape the length of the baking tin. Prove the dough for 1–1½ hours in a warm, draught-free room until the dough doubles in size.

- Bake in a preheated oven at 200°C for 25–30 minutes until the top turns golden brown.

 Final moulding is important for the texture of the bread. The dough must be moulded tightly with an even pressure without damaging the gluten matrix. It should be placed in tins with the seam at the bottom to allow the dough to expand fully.

Clockwise from top: Raisin Bread, Cinnamon Roll.

Savarin

Ingredients:
Ferment

Strong flour (bread flour)	40 g
Instant dry yeast	6 g
Milk	110 g, warmed to 38°C
Sugar	50 g

Dough

Strong flour (bread flour)	160 g
Plain flour (all-purpose flour)	200 g
Salt	4 g
Eggs	290 g (5, large)
Butter	170 g, melted and cooled

Method:

- With an electric mixer with a whisk, prepare the ferment by mixing the 4 ingredients on medium speed for 3 minutes. Ferment the mixture for 20–30 minutes in a container at about 27°C. The ferment is ready when it rises and begins to fall. This indicates that the ferment is matured.

- To prepare the dough, use a paddle to beat the eggs and flour on medium speed for 2 minutes until well blended. Add the ferment and continue mixing on medium speed for 2 minutes. Melt butter and add to the dough on slow speed for 1 minute. Allow the dough to ferment in a warm place for 30 minutes.

- Grease 6-cm wide savarin moulds with butter, dust them with flour and half fill them with the dough. Prove in a warm place for 30 minutes and bake in a preheated oven at 200°C for 20 minutes until golden brown.

- Prepare syrup by boiling 500 g of water and 300 g of sugar together. When the sugar has melted completely, allow the syrup to cool. When it is lukewarm, stir in 100 g of rum. Dip the baked savarins into the syrup. When cool, pipe fresh cream into the center and top with fresh fruits.

Chef's Tip: As the dough resembles batter, it can be easily piped into the savarin moulds from a piping bag. For larger savarins, bake at 180°C for 25 minutes. This recipe can be adapted to make babas. Mix in 160 g of mixed fruit after adding the butter.

Almond Gugelhopf

Ingredients:

Strong white flour (bread flour)	500 g
Milk powder	15 g
Bread improver	8 g
Instant dry yeast	8 g
Sugar	75 g
Salt	8 g
Eggs	175g (3, medium)
Cold water	100 g
Butter	200 g, softened
Raisins	250 g

Method:

- With an electric mixer and dough hook at slow speed, blend the dry ingredients together for 1 minute. Add eggs then cold water and continue mixing on slow speed for another minute. Change to medium speed and mix for 5 minutes until dough is half developed.

- Add softened butter in 5 portions over 7–10 minutes on medium speed until dough is fully developed. Fold in raisins by mixing on slow speed for 1 minute.

- Transfer the dough onto a flour-dusted work surface and round up dough with both hands. Place dough into an airtight container and let it rise in the refrigerator for 8 hours or overnight until dough doubles in bulk.

- Divide the dough into 3 pieces of 440 g each. Mould the dough into smooth round balls and leave for 10 minutes. Prepare 3 gugelhopf tins by brushing butter and coating with almond flakes.

- Round up the dough pieces and make a hole in the centre. Place into gugelhopf pans. Prove in a warm place for 1 hour until dough doubles in size. Place the pans on a baking tray and bake in a preheated oven at 190°C for 25–30 minutes until glossy and golden. Turn out and cool on a wire rack. Dust with confectioners' sugar.

Chef's Tip: This bread is very rich and tasty. The butter is 40 percent that of flour. Due to the high fat content, butter must be added slowly to the dough. This dough is best kept cool during processing for easy handling and moulding.

Cottage Pan Rings

Ingredients:

Ferment

Strong flour (bread flour)	40 g
Milk powder	11 g
Instant dry yeast	12 g
Sugar	5 g
Eggs	80 g (1½, medium)
Water	170 g, warmed to 42°C

Dough

Strong flour (bread flour)	200 g
Plain flour (all-purpose flour)	160 g
Bread improver	6 g
Salt	4 g
Brown sugar	65 g
Shortening	65 g

Filling

Brown sugar	190 g
Butter	190 g, softened
Raisins	110 g

Method:

- With an electric mixer and whisk, prepare the ferment by mixing the ingredients on medium speed for 3 minutes. Ferment the mixture for 20–30 minutes in a container at about 27°C. The ferment is ready when it rises and begins to fall.

To further improve the flavour of the bread, replace shortening with butter. The use of all-purpose flour in this recipe results in a smaller dough, but the quality and tenderness is better.

- To prepare the dough, combine the dry ingredients with the ferment and mix on medium speed for 3 minutes. Add shortening and continue to mix on medium speed for 8–10 minutes until dough is fully developed.

- Round up and rest the dough for 20 minutes. Roll dough out into a 1-cm thick sheet. Mix brown sugar and softened butter and spread over dough sheet. Sprinkle with raisins.

- Roll up as for Swiss roll and brush all over with melted butter. Cut into 2.5 cm wide slices and place flat down in prepared 15 cm round pans. Each pan should accommodate about 6 slices.

- Prove for 1 hour until doubled in size. Brush beaten egg over the dough and bake in a preheated oven at 190°C for 20–25 minutes until golden brown. Turn out and leave to cool on a wire rack.

Almond Kuchen

Ingredients:

Strong white flour (bread flour)	500 g
Bread improver	8 g
Instant dry yeast	14 g
Sugar	70 g
Salt	8 g
Cold milk	290 g
Butter	125 g, softened
Raisins	140 g

Method:

- With an electric mixer and dough hook, mix the dry ingredients for 1 minute on low speed. Add cold milk and mix on low speed for another minute. Increase to medium speed to develop the dough for 3 minutes and add butter. Continue mixing for 10 minutes until dough is fully developed. Mix in raisins on low speed for 1 minute.

- Round up dough and place into an airtight container to rise in a warm place for 1 hour until dough is double in bulk. Roll out the dough to a rectangle 1-cm thick. Fill with almond filling (*see recipe*) and prove in a warm place for about 40–50 minutes.

- Bake in a preheated oven at 200°C for 20–25 minutes.

Almond Filling

Ingredients:

Butter	225 g
Sugar	200 g
Almond flakes	150 g
Ground cinnamon	1 g
Candied red cherries	30 g
Candied green cherries	30 g
Eggs	150 g (3, small), beaten

Method

- Cook butter and sugar in a pan for a few minutes. Add almond flakes, ground cinnamon and cherries. Allow mixture to cool for 5–10 minutes and fold in the eggs.

- Spread the filling evenly over the rolled out dough.

 For the dough, 290 g cold milk can be replaced with 30 g milk powder and 260 g water. Milk or water must be cold to maintain the temperature of the dough at 27–30°C.

From left: Cottage Pan Rings, Almond Kuchen.

Veggie Bread

Ingredients:
Sponge

Strong white flour (bread flour)	350 g
Water	210 g
Salt	2 g
A pinch of Instant dry yeast	

Dough

Strong white flour (bread flour)	150 g
Bread improver	8 g
Dry wheat gluten	30 g
Instant dry yeast	12 g
Sugar	60 g
Salt	5 g
Ground black pepper	3 g
Tomato puree	30 g
Shortening	50 g
Carrot	100 g, shredded
Celery	75 g, chopped
Fried onion	50 g
Green and red capsicums	200 g, diced

Method:
- With an electric mixer and dough hook, prepare the sponge by mixing the sponge ingredients on low speed for 3 minutes. The sponge should be firm, dry and cool (24°C) to the touch. Ferment the sponge overnight for 12–15 hours in an airtight container at about 27°C.

The dough must be moulded to the length of the bread tin. This allows for proper expansion of the dough. The tins must also be greased lightly to allow for the easy release of the bread after baking.

- When the sponge is ready, prepare the dough. Place the remaining dry ingredients into the mixer and mix on low speed. Add tomato puree. Immediately cut the sponge into a few pieces and add to the mixture over 1 minute. Increase to medium speed and mix for 2 minutes. Add shortening and mix for another 5–7 minutes. Mix in the rest of the ingredients on low speed for 1 minute until well blended.

- Round up and rest the dough for 10 minutes. Divide into 4 pieces, each 270 g and round up. Leave dough to rest for 10 minutes. Flatten slightly with the palm of your hand and roll out with a rolling pin. Mould the dough pieces into a cylindrical shape.

- Prove in a warm place for 40–50 minutes until the dough doubles in size. Bake in a preheated oven at 200°C for 12–15 minutes until the bread turns golden brown.

Celery Bread

Ingredients:

Strong white flour (bread flour)	500 g
Bread improver	8 g
Instant dry yeast	13 g
Sugar	65 g
Salt	8 g
Milk powder	20 g
Celery powder	5 g
Egg	40 g (1, small)
Cold water	240 g
Shortening	50 g
Chopped celery	150 g

Method:
- With an electric mixer and dough hook at low speed, blend the dry ingredients together for 1 minute. Add egg then water and mix on low speed for another minute. Increase to medium speed, mix for 5 minutes and add shortening. Continue to mix for another 7–10 minutes until dough is fully developed. Mix in chopped celery on low speed over 1 minute.

- Transfer the dough onto a flour-dusted work surface and round up dough with both hands. Place dough into an airtight container and let it rise in a warm place for 1 hour until dough is double in bulk.

- Divide the dough into 4 portions of 275 g each. Round up and rest dough for 15 minutes. Press down and roll the dough out with a rolling pin. Mould firmly with the fingertips into a cylindrical shape, the length of the baking tin.

- Prove dough for 1 hour in a warm, draught-free room until dough doubles in size. Bake in a preheated oven at 200°C for 25–30 minutes until the top turns golden brown.

The volume of the moulded dough should be one-third to half the volume of the bread tin to produce a good-looking loaf of bread. If oven space is insufficient to bake 4 loaves, 2 loaves can be retarded in the refrigerator prior to proving. They can be removed after 1/2–1 hour and proved as usual.

From front: Veggie Bread, Celery Bread.

Potato Cheese Bread

Ingredients:

Strong white flour (bread flour)	400 g
Potato flakes or granules	100 g
Milk powder	25 g
Bread improver	8 g
Instant dry yeast	10 g
Dry wheat gluten	10 g
Parmesan cheese	25 g
Sugar	15 g
Salt	5 g
Eggs	150 g (3, small)
Cold water	280 g
Butter	50 g, softened

Topping
Sesame seeds

Method:

- With an electric mixer and dough hook at low speed, blend the dry ingredients together for 1 minute. Add eggs then water and mix on low speed for another minute. Increase to medium speed and mix for 5 minutes until the dough is half developed. Add softened butter in 3 portions and mix on medium speed for 7–10 minutes until the dough is fully developed.

- Transfer the dough onto a flour-dusted work surface and round up the dough with both hands. Place the dough into an airtight container and let it rise in a warm place for 1 hour until the dough is double in bulk.

- Divide the dough into 2 pieces and round up tightly with the palm of your hand. Leave for 10 minutes, round up the dough pieces and flatten with a rolling pin. Prick the dough pieces with a fork to prevent them from bulging up when proving.

- Allow the dough to prove for about 1 hour until doubled in size. Brush the tops with egg glaze and sprinkle with sesame seeds. Bake in a preheated oven at 220°C for 18–20 minutes until golden brown. Turn out and cool on a wire rack.

 Chef's Tip: This bread is ideal for making sandwiches. The addition of dry wheat gluten increases the volume of the bread. Dry wheat gluten is usually added to breads with large amounts of seeds, nuts, bran and other types of flour.

Potato Bread

Ingredients:

Strong white flour (bread flour)	425 g
Potato flakes or granules	75 g
Milk powder	10 g
Bread improver	8 g
Instant dry yeast	13 g
Sugar	100 g
Salt	3 g
Eggs	150 g (3, small)
Cold water	165 g
Butter	100 g, softened

Topping
Custard*

Method:

- With an electric mixer and dough hook at low speed, blend the dry ingredients together for 1 minute. Add eggs then water and mix on low speed for another minute. Increase to medium speed and mix for 5 minutes until the dough is half developed. Add softened butter in 3 portions and mix on medium speed for 7–10 minutes until the dough is fully developed.

- Transfer the dough onto a flour-dusted work surface and round up the dough with both hands. Place the dough into an airtight container and let it rise in a warm place for 1 hour until the dough is double in bulk.

- Divide the dough into 50 g pieces and round up tightly with the palm of your hand. Leave for 10 minutes and round up the dough pieces. Place 6 of the dough pieces together in 2 rows of 3.

- Allow the dough to prove for about 1 hour until the dough doubles in size. Brush the tops with egg glaze and pipe crosses on each dough piece with custard. Bake in a preheated oven at 200°C for 15–20 minutes until glossy and golden. Turn out and cool on a wire rack.

* Use ready-made custard or instant custard powder. Follow the manufacturer's instructions on the packaging.

 Chef's Tip: When using fresh potatoes instead of potato flakes, mash up 280 g of boiled potatoes and refrigerate. Reduce to using 1 egg and omit the water from the formulation as fresh potatoes contain 75 percent water.

From left: Potato Cheese Bread, Potato Bread.

Sweet Corn Bread

Ingredients:

Sponge

Strong white flour (bread flour)	350 g
Instant dry yeast	4 g
Water	210 g

Dough

Strong white flour (bread flour)	150 g
Milk powder	15 g
Bread improver	8 g
Instant dry yeast	8 g
Sugar	60 g
Salt	10 g
Water	75 g
Butter	60 g
Sweet corn (canned)	250 g

Method:

- With an electric mixer and dough hook, prepare the sponge by mixing the 3 ingredients on low speed for 3 minutes. The sponge should be firm, dry and cool (24°C) to the touch. Ferment the sponge for 4–5 hours in an airtight container at about 27°C.

- When the sponge is ready, prepare the dough. Place the remaining dry ingredients into the mixer. Add water and mix on low speed. Immediately cut sponge into a few pieces and add to the mixture over 1 minute. Increase speed to medium and mix for 2 minutes. Add butter and mix for another 5 minutes. Fold in sweet corn on low speed for 1 minute until well blended.

- Round up and rest the dough for 10 minutes. Divide the dough into 300 g pieces and mould round. Rest for 10 minutes to allow the dough pieces to recover. Roll out the dough pieces and mould them into a cylindrical shape to fit the tin. Prove in a warm place for 1 hour until dough doubles in volume.

- Bake in a preheated oven at 200°C for 25 minutes until the bread turns golden brown.

Chef's Tip: This recipe makes 4 loaves of bread. If your oven can only accommodate 2 loaves, place the other 2 loaves in the refrigerator for at least 1/2 hour before proving. The dough can also be placed in the refrigerator overnight and proved the next day, provided the temperature is below 5°C and the dough is properly covered to prevent drying.

Prune and Walnut Bread

Ingredients:

Strong white flour (bread flour)	360 g
Wheat bran	40 g
Milk powder	20 g
Dry wheat gluten	12 g
Bread improver	6 g
Instant dry yeast	10 g
Mixed spice	4 g
Sugar	55 g
Salt	6 g
Egg	50 g (1, small)
Cold water	200 g
Butter	55 g
Prunes	120 g, chopped
Walnuts	60 g, chopped

Coating
Wheat bran

Method

- With an electric mixer and dough hook at low speed, blend the dry ingredients together for 1 minute. Add water and egg and mix on low speed for another minute. Put in butter and mix on medium speed for 12–15 minutes. Premix prunes and walnuts and add on low speed over 1 minute until evenly mixed.

- Transfer the dough onto a flour-dusted work surface and round up the dough with both hands. Place the dough into an airtight container and let it rise in a warm place for 1 hour until the dough doubles in size.

- Divide the dough into 3 pieces, each weighing 330 g. Round up and rest the dough pieces for 15 minutes. Press down and roll the dough pieces out with a rolling pin. Mould each piece firmly with the fingertips into a cylindrical shape the length of the baking tin. Wet the surface and coat with wheat bran.

- Prove the dough for 1 hour in a warm, draught-free room until the dough doubles in size. Bake in a preheated oven at 200°C for 25–30 minutes until the tops turns golden brown.

 Chef's Tip: Dry wheat gluten can be substituted with wet gluten. Wet gluten is prepared by mixing 100 g bread flour, 65 g water and a pinch of salt. Immerse the dough in water for 20 minutes and wash out all the starch from it. This will yield about 36 g of wet gluten and is equivalent to 12 g of dry wheat gluten needed for this recipe.

Lemon Poppy Seed Plait

Ingredients:

Strong white flour (bread flour)	300 g
Plain flour (all-purpose flour)	200 g
Milk powder	25 g
Bread improver	8 g
Instant dry yeast	10 g
Sugar	40 g
Salt	9 g
Egg	50 g (1, small)
Water	250 g
Butter	40 g, softened
Lemon flavouring	5 g
Poppy seeds	25 g

Method:

- With an electric mixer and dough hook, mix all the dry ingredients for 1 minute on low speed. Add egg and water and mix on low speed for another minute. Increase to medium speed and develop the dough for 3 minutes. Add butter, lemon flavouring and poppy seeds. Continue mixing for 10 minutes until the dough is fully developed.

- Round up the dough and place into an airtight container. Leave the dough to rise in a warm place for 1 hour until doubled in bulk. Divide the dough into 50 g pieces. Round up the dough pieces and let rest for 10 minutes.

- Flatten the dough pieces with a rolling pin and mould the dough such that the centre is thicker than the edges. The dough pieces should ideally be 20-cm long. Join 5 strands of dough at the top from left to right. Plait by placing the strands in the following order, 2 over 3, 5 over 2 and 1 over 3. Repeat the sequence until the plait is completed.

- Prove the plaits in a warm place for about 1 hour. Brush beaten egg over the surface and sprinkle poppy seeds over it. Bake in a preheated oven at 190°C for 20–25 minutes.

Before plaiting, make sure each strand of dough is moulded tight with the ends thinner than the centre. This will give character to the plait and prevent the plait from shrinking after baking.

Oat Bran Bread

Ingredients:
Sponge

Strong flour (bread flour)	350 g
Instant dry yeast	4 g
Water	210 g

Dough

Strong flour (bread flour)	75 g
Oat bran	75 g
Bread improver	8 g
Instant dry yeast	6 g
Salt	10 g
Milk	50 g
Water	70 g
Shortening	15 g

Coating
Rolled oats

Method:

- With an electric mixer and dough hook, prepare the sponge by mixing the 3 ingredients on low speed for 3 minutes. The sponge should be firm, dry and cool (24°C) to the touch. Ferment the sponge for 4–5 hours in an airtight container at about 27°C.

- When the sponge is ready, prepare the dough. Place the remaining dry ingredients into the mixer. Add milk and water and mix on low speed. Immediately cut sponge into a few pieces and add to the mixture over 1 minute. Increase speed to medium and mix for 2 minutes. Add shortening and mix for another 7–10 minutes until the dough is fully developed.

- Round up the dough and rest on a flour-dusted work surface for 15 minutes. Divide dough into 3 pieces each weighing 290 g. Round up and rest the dough pieces for 15 minutes. Press down and roll each dough piece out with a rolling pin. Mould it firmly with your fingertips into a cylindrical shape, the length of the tin.

- Wet the surface of the dough pieces and coat with rolled oats. Prove the dough for 1 hour in a warm place until the dough doubles in size. Bake in a preheated oven at 230°C for 25 minutes until golden brown.

This bread can be baked with steam during the first 12 minutes of baking. Baking with steam will give the bread better volume and a crispy crust. Oat bran can also be used to coat the surface of the bread.

From front: Lemon Poppy Seed Plait, Oat Bran Bread.

Pumpkin Bread

Ingredients:

Strong white flour (bread flour)	500 g
Milk powder	20 g
Bread improver	8 g
Instant dry yeast	14 g
Sugar	110 g
Salt	8 g
Mixed spice	2 g
Pumpkin paste	450 g
Eggs	100 g (2, small)
Cold water	70 g
Shortening	100 g

Method:

- With an electric mixer and dough hook at low speed, blend the dry ingredients together for about 1 minute. Add 150 g of pumpkin paste, eggs and water and mix on low speed for another minute. Put in shortening and mix on medium speed for 12 minutes until the dough is fully developed.

- Transfer the dough onto a flour-dusted work surface and round up the dough with both hands. Place the dough into an airtight container and let it rise in a warm place for 1 hour until the dough is double in bulk.

- Divide the dough into 3 pieces, each 350 g and mould round. Leave for 10 minutes. With a rolling pin, flatten dough into a sheet 30-cm wide. Spread with remaining pumpkin paste and roll the dough up like a Swiss roll. Stretch the roll slightly and fold in half. Give the roll 2 or 3 twists and place into a tin.

- Prove the dough in a warm, draught-free place for 1 hour Bake in a preheated oven at 200°C for 25 minutes.

Sweet Potato Bread

Ingredients:

Strong white flour (bread flour)	400 g
Milk powder	25 g
Bread improver	6 g
Instant dry yeast	10 g
Dry wheat gluten	8 g
Sugar	50 g
Salt	6 g
Sweet potato	400 g, cooked and mashed
Egg	70 g (1, large)
Cold water	30 g
Butter	50 g, softened

Method:

- With an electric mixer and dough hook at low speed, blend the dry ingredients together for 1 minute. Add sweet potato, egg and water and mix on low speed for another minute. Increase to medium speed and mix for 5 minutes. Add softened butter in 3 portions and mix on medium speed for 7–10 minutes until the dough is fully developed.

- Transfer the dough onto a flour-dusted work surface and round up the dough with both hands. Place the dough into an airtight container and let it rise in a warm place for 1 hour until the dough doubles in size.

- Divide the dough into 50 g pieces and round up tightly with the palm of your hand. Leave for 10 minutes and round up the dough pieces again. Place 6 pieces together in 2 rows of 3s. Allow the dough to prove for about 1 hour until the dough doubles in size.

- Brush the tops with egg glaze. Using custard, pipe lines across the 2 rows of dough pieces to form a cross on each dough piece. Bake in a preheated oven at 200°C for 15–20 minutes until glossy and golden brown. Turn out and cool on a wire rack.

The sweet potato must be steamed, mashed and chilled prior to adding into the dough. The orange coloured variety of sweet potato should be used as it gives good colour and flavour to the product.

The pumpkin paste can be easily prepared by cooking pumpkin (steamed and mashed) with some sugar until it forms a paste that is easy to spread. Add sugar according to your taste.

From front: Sweet Potato Bread, Pumpkin Bread.

Carrot and Honey Bread

Ingredients:

Strong white flour (bread flour)	450 g
Milk powder	15 g
Bread improver	7 g
Instant dry yeast	9 g
Salt	9 g
Honey	70 g
Cold carrot juice	260 g
Butter	35 g, softened
Carrot	90 g, chilled and shredded

Method:

- With an electric mixer and dough hook at low speed, blend the dry ingredients together for 1–2 minutes. Add honey then carrot juice and mix on low speed for another 2 minutes. Increase to medium speed and mix for 5 minutes. Gradually blend in butter and carrot shreds and mix for another 7–10 minutes until dough is fully developed.

- Transfer the dough onto a flour-dusted work surface and round up dough with both hands. Place dough into an airtight container and let it rise in a warm place for 1 hour until dough doubles in size.

- Divide the dough into 3 pieces, 310 g each. Round up and leave for 15 minutes. Press down and roll the dough out with a rolling pin. Mould it firmly with the fingertips into a cylindrical shape, the length of the baking tin. Grease the tins and place the dough inside, with the seam facing down.

- Prove dough for 1 hour in a draught-free room until dough doubles in size. Proving may take longer if the room is cold. Bake in a preheated oven at 200°C for 25 minutes until the top turns golden brown.

Chef's Tip:

To check whether the bread is baked, it is best to take out one loaf of bread from the oven. Using a spatula, scrape around the tin to make sure the bread is not sticking to the sides. If the sides and bottom of the bread has turned golden brown, then it is properly baked. If the sides of the bread is pale but the top is brown, quickly return to the tin and cover the top with greaseproof paper or aluminium foil to prevent the top from burning. At the same time reduce the top heat.

Cheese and Onion Bread

Ingredients:

Strong white flour (bread flour)	400 g
Milk powder	20 g
Bread improver	6 g
Instant dry yeast	8 g
Sugar	40 g
Salt	8 g
Cold water	240 g
Butter	40 g, softened
Fried onions	120 g
Parmesan cheese	12 g, grated

Topping

Cheddar cheese	80 g, grated
Poppy seeds	

Method:

- With an electric mixer and dough hook at low speed, blend the dry ingredients together for 1 minute. Add water and mix on low speed for another minute. Increase to medium speed and mix for 5 minutes. Add softened butter mix for 7–10 minutes. Fold in fried onions and parmesan cheese and mix on low speed for 1 minute.

- Transfer the dough onto a flour-dusted work surface and round up the dough with both hands. Place the dough into an airtight container and let it rise in a warm place for 1 hour until dough is double in bulk.

- Divide the dough into 40 g pieces. Mould the pieces of dough into smooth round balls. Leave for 10 minutes, round up the dough pieces and place them into round 18-cm tins. Place 6 around and 1 in the centre of each tin. Cover the tins and prove for 1 hour until the dough has doubled in size.

- Brush the tops with egg glaze and sprinkle cheddar cheese and poppy seeds over them. Place the tins on a baking tray and bake in a preheated oven at 200°C for 20 minutes until glossy and golden brown. Turn out and cool on a wire rack.

Chef's Tip: Baking tins must be properly greased so that the bread can be easily removed. Lining the tins with paper is not advisable, as the paper will stick to the bread after baking. Rounding up the dough twice after scaling results in dough with a smooth surface and good volume.

Wholemeal Bread

Ingredients:

Strong white flour (bread flour)	415 g
Wheat bran	75 g
Wheat germ	12 g
Milk powder	5 g
Bread improver	8 g
Instant dry yeast	7 g
Salt	10 g
Egg	30 g (½, medium)
Cold water	330 g
Shortening	15 g

Method:

- With an electric mixer and dough hook at low speed, blend the dry ingredients together for 1 minute. Add egg and water and mix on low speed for another minute. Put in shortening and mix on medium speed for 12–15 minutes until the dough is fully developed.

- Transfer the dough onto a flour-dusted work surface and round up the dough with both hands. Place the dough into an airtight container and let it rise in a warm place for 1 hour until the dough doubles in size.

- Divide the dough into 3 pieces, each weighing 300 g. Round up and rest the dough pieces for 15 minutes. Press down and roll the dough out with a rolling pin. Gently with the tips of your fingers, mould tightly by bringing the dough from the edges to the centre. This will create an oval shaped dough with the ends tapering, resembling a lemon.

- Prove the dough for 1 hour in a warm, draught-free room until the dough doubles in size. Make 2 cuts on the surface to allow full expansion during baking.

- Preheat the oven to 230°C. Bake with a tray of water to generate steam for 10–12 minutes. Open the door of the oven to release the steam and remove any water remaining. Continue to bake for another 10 minutes until the bread is golden brown. Cool on a wire rack.

A mixture of wheat bran, wheat germ and strong flour has been used as a substitute for wholemeal flour. This mixture will produce a loaf with better volume and softer texture. By further substituting wheat bran with oat bran, rice bran and barley bran, many types of nutritious breads can be produced.

Sandwich Bread

Ingredients:

Sponge

Strong white flour (bread flour)	350 g
Instant dry yeast	4 g
Water	210 g

Dough

Strong white flour (bread flour)	150 g
Milk powder	15 g
Bread improver	8 g
Instant dry yeast	8 g
Sugar	30 g
Salt	10 g
Water	100 g
Shortening	30 g

Method:

- With an electric mixer and dough hook, prepare the sponge by mixing the 3 ingredients on low speed for 3 minutes. The sponge should be firm, dry and cool (24°C) to the touch. Ferment the sponge for 4–5 hours in an airtight container at about 27°C.

- When the sponge is ready, prepare the dough. Place the remaining dry ingredients into the mixer. Add water and mix on low speed. Immediately cut the sponge into a few pieces and add to the mixture over 1 minute. Increase to medium speed and mix for 2 minutes. Add shortening and mix for another 5–7 minutes until the dough is fully developed.

- Round up and rest the dough for 10 minutes. Divide the dough into 2 pieces and round up. Leave for 10 minutes and roll out the dough with a rolling pin. Mould into a cylindrical shape about twice the length of the bread tin. Cut the dough into 3 equal pieces and place in tins side by side.

- Prove in a warm place for 1 hour until the dough rises to a height of about 1 cm from the top of the tin. Place a greased cover over the tin and bake in a preheated oven at 230°C for 25–30 minutes until the bread turns golden brown.

Fermenting the sponge for 4–5 hours will result in a bread with superior taste, aroma, softness and extended shelf life. Cutting the dough and placing it crosswise in the tin produces bread with excellent grain and texture.

From front: Wholemeal Bread, Sandwich Bread.

Brown Coburg

Ingredients:

Strong white flour (bread flour)	425 g
Wheat bran	75 g
Milk powder	5 g
Bread improver	8 g
Instant dry yeast	8 g
Salt	10 g
Cold water	330 g
Shortening	5 g

Method:

- With an electric mixer and dough hook at low speed, blend the dry ingredients together for about 1 minute. Add water and mix on low speed for another minute. Put in shortening and mix on medium speed for 12–15 minutes until dough is fully developed.

- Transfer the dough onto a flour-dusted work surface and round up dough with both hands. Place dough into an airtight container and let it rise in a warm place for 1 hour until dough is double in bulk.

- Divide the dough into 2 pieces of 420 g each and mould round. Leave for 10 minutes. Remould the dough pieces and form them into balls. Place the dough pieces onto a lightly greased tray.

- Prove in a warm, draught-free and humid place for 1 hour until double in bulk. Cut a cross 1-cm deep across the top of the dough piece.

- Preheat the oven to 230°C. Bake with a tray of water to generate steam for the first 10 minutes of the baking time. Open the door of the oven and remove any water remaining. Continue to bake for 10–15 minutes. Cool on a wire rack.

This recipe is also suitable for making wholemeal sandwich bread. The dough is shaped into a baton and put into the tin with the seam down. The lid is put on when the dough rises to 90% the height of the tin and baked immediately.

Swiss Brown

Ingredients:

Strong white flour (bread flour)	500 g
Instant dry yeast	8 g
Bread improver	8 g
Sugar	15 g
Salt	10 g
Treacle	5 g
Cold water	310 g
Shortening	15 g
Caraway seeds	5 g

Method:

- With an electric mixer and dough hook at low speed, blend the ingredients except caraway seeds together for 1 minute. Increase to medium speed and mix for 5 minutes. Add caraway seeds and mix for 7–10 minutes until dough is fully developed.

- Transfer the dough onto a flour-dusted work surface and round up the dough with both hands. Place the dough into an airtight container and let it rise in a warm place for 1–1½ hours until the dough doubles in size.

- Divide the dough into 2 pieces, each 425 g. Round up the dough and leave for 15 minutes. Flatten the dough with a rolling pin. Mould the dough tightly with your fingertips from the top downwards and from the sides inwards making certain that the centre is thicker than the edges.

Generally, fat is added to the dough mixture after it has absorbed all the water and has formed dough. However, if only a little fat is needed, it can be added together with the other ingredients. Baking with steam only half way through the entire baking process allows the dough to set and turn golden brown.

- Prove the dough in a warm, draught-free place for 1–1½ hours. Make a cut through the centre of the dough and bake with a tray of water to generate steam at 230°C for 10 minutes. Open the door of the oven and remove any water remaining. Continue to bake for a minimum of 10 minutes until the bread is golden brown.

From front: Brown Coburg, Swiss Brown.

Traditional Rye Bread

Ingredients:

Rye flour	350 g
Strong white flour (bread flour)	150 g
Dark malt flour	5 g
Bread improver	8 g
Instant dry yeast	8 g
Dry wheat sour	13 g
Salt	10 g
Cold water	390 g

Method:

- With an electric mixer and dough hook at low speed, blend the dry ingredients together for about 1 minute. Add water and mix on low speed for 7–10 minutes.

- Transfer the dough onto a flour-dusted work surface and round up with both hands. Place dough into an airtight container and let it rise in a warm place for 20 minutes.

- Divide the dough into 2 pieces, each 450 g and mould round. Leave for 10 minutes. Remould the dough pieces and shape them into long cylindrical shapes or round shapes.

- Prove the dough in a warm, draught-free place for 30–40 minutes. Carefully turn the dough pieces onto a lightly greased or greaseproof paper-lined tray.

- Preheat the oven to 250°C. Bake with a tray of water to generate steam for 45 minutes. After 20 minutes, reduce the oven temperature to 220°C and continue to bake. During the last 5 minutes of baking time, open the door of the oven to release steam and remove any water remaining. After baking, transfer onto a cooling rack.

Continental Rye Bread

Ingredients:

Strong white flour (bread flour)	350 g
Rye flour	100 g
Roasted malt flour	10 g
Wheat bran	50 g
Dry wheat sour*	13 g
Bread improver	8 g
Instant dry yeast	6 g
Salt	5 g
Caraway seeds	5 g
Cold water	340 g
Shortening	10 g

Method:

- With an electric mixer and dough hook at low speed, blend the dry ingredients together for about 1 minute. Add water and mix on low speed for another minute. Put in shortening and mix for 8–10 minutes on low speed until the dough is fully developed.

- Transfer the dough onto a flour-dusted work surface and round up with both hands. Place dough into an airtight container and let it rise in a warm place for 20 minutes.

- Divide the dough into 2 pieces, each 420 g and mould round. Leave for 10 minutes. Remould each dough piece into a baton shape. Place on semolina or sugi flour dusted trays. Prove dough in a warm, draught-free place for 40–50 minutes. Make 2 cuts across the surface of the dough pieces.

- Preheat the oven to 225°C. Bake with a tray of water to generate steam for 15 minutes. Open the door of the oven to release steam and remove any water remaining. Continue to bake for another 20–25 minutes.

* **Dry wheat sour is available from baking specialty shops.**

This recipe produces a rye bread with a delicious aroma of caraway seeds. The caraway seeds should be crushed with a rolling pin to release the aromatic compounds prior to adding to the dough. Dark treacle can be used as a substitute for roasted malt flour.

This recipe produces a rye bread that is slightly heavy but moist and full of flavour. You may serve the loaves in wicker baskets for an authentic look. If using wicker baskets, sprinkle them with lots of rye flour. Rye bread is best baked on the hearth of the oven with lots of steam.

Clockwise from right: Continental Rye Bread, Traditional Rye Bread (long and round).

German Muesli Bread

Ingredients:

Strong white flour (bread flour)	280 g
Multigrain	80 g, plus extra for coating
Wheat bran	40 g
Dry wheat gluten	12 g
Bread improver	6 g
Instant dry yeast	8 g
Sugar	30 g
Salt	8 g
Cold water	260 g
Butter	30 g
Raisins	120 g
Chopped walnuts	100 g

Method:
- With an electric mixer and dough hook at low speed, mix the dry ingredients together for 1 minute. Add water and mix on low speed for 2 minutes. Put in butter and mix on medium speed for 12–15 minutes until dough is fully developed. Premix raisins and walnuts and add on low speed over 1 minute making sure not to crush the raisins.

You can prepare your own multigrain by mixing together equal proportions of rolled oats, barley bran, rice bran, corn meal, millet, flaxseeds, sesame seeds and poppy seeds. You may add other seeds and grains to this combination or omit any as desired.

- Transfer the dough onto a flour-dusted work surface and round up the dough with both hands. Place the dough into an airtight container and let it rise in a warm place for 1 hour until the dough doubles up in size.

- Divide the dough into 3 pieces, each 350 g. Leave for 15 minutes. Press down and roll the dough pieces out with a rolling pin. Mould each piece firmly with your fingertips into a cylindrical shape, the length of the baking tin. Wet the surface and coat with multigrain.

- Prove the dough pieces for 1 hour in a warm, draught-free room until the dough doubles in size. Bake at 200°C for 25 minutes.

Milk and Cheese Plait

Ingredients:

Strong white flour (bread flour)	500 g
Milk powder	75 g
Bread improver	8 g
Instant dry yeast	4 g
Sugar	70 g
Salt	9 g
Water	310 g
Butter	40 g, softened

Topping
Cheddar cheese	grated

Method:
- With an electric mixer and dough hook, mix the dry ingredients for 1 minute on low speed. Add water and mix on low speed for another minute. Increase to medium speed to develop the dough for 3 minutes and add butter. Continue mixing for 10 minutes until dough is fully developed.

- Round up dough and place into an airtight container to rise in a warm place for 1 hour until dough is double in bulk. Divide dough into 50 g pieces. Round up the dough and leave for 10 minutes.

- To braid a loaf, roll out 4 pieces of dough into 20-cm long strips. The strips should be thinner on the ends and thicker in the middle. Place the 4 strips with the tips at one end touching. Weave the strips together to form a braid. This is done by weaving strip 2 over strip 3, strip 4 over strip 2 and strip 1 over strip 3. This is repeated until the braid is completed.

- Prove the braid in a warm place for about 1 hour. Brush beaten egg over the surface and sprinkle cheddar cheese over it. Bake in a preheated oven at 190°C for 20–25 minutes.

The dough is fully proved when it has doubled in size and springs back slowly when lightly pressed with the fingers.

From left: German Muesli Bread, Milk and Cheese Plait.

Malt Bread

Ingredients:

Strong white flour (bread flour)	450 g
Malt flour	100 g
Wheat bran	50 g
Bread improver	8 g
Instant dry yeast	14 g
Salt	10 g
Treacle	25 g
Cold water	320 g
Shortening	10 g
Raisins	175 g

Method:

- With an electric mixer and dough hook at low speed, blend the dry ingredients together for about 1 minute. Add treacle then water and mix on low speed for another minute. Put in shortening and mix on medium speed for 12 minutes until dough is fully developed. Mix in the raisins on low speed for 1 minute.

- Transfer the dough onto a flour-dusted work surface and round up the dough with both hands. Place the dough into an airtight container and let it rise in a warm place for 1 hour until dough is double in bulk.

- Divide the dough into 4 pieces, each 290 g and mould round. Leave for 10 minutes. Remould the dough pieces and form them into cylindrical shapes. Prove dough in a warm, draught-free place for 1 hour.

- Place the dough pieces into lightly greased tins with the seam facing downwards. Bake in a preheated oven at 190°C for 30–40 minutes. Cool on a wire rack.

Treacle imparts a nice flavour and colour to the bread. It can be substituted with molasses or caramel. Malt flour is mostly maltose (malt sugar). This sugar will caramelise during baking. It will darken the crust in the early stage of baking if the oven temperature is set too high.

Wheat Germ Bread

Ingredients:

Strong white flour (bread flour)	425 g
Wheat germ	75 g
Milk powder	15 g
Instant dry yeast	9 g
Bread improver	8 g
Sugar	30 g
Salt	10 g
Cold water	340 g
Shortening	30 g

Method:

- With an electric mixer and dough hook at low speed, blend the dry ingredients together for 1 minute. Add water and mix on low speed for 2 minutes. Put in shortening and mix on medium speed for 12–15 minutes until the dough is fully developed.

- Transfer the dough onto a lightly floured work surface and round up the dough with both hands. Place the dough into an airtight container and let it rise in a warm place for 1 hour until the dough doubles in size.

- Divide dough into 3 pieces, each 300 g. Round up the dough pieces and leave for 10 minutes. Press down and roll dough out with a rolling pin. Gently, with the tips of your fingers, mould tightly by bringing the dough from the top downward to resemble a Swiss roll. Grease the baking tins and place the dough inside with the seam downwards.

- Prove the dough for 1 hour in a warm, draught-free room until the dough doubles in size. Bake in a preheated oven at 220°C for 25 minutes.

It is important to rest the dough after rounding it up prior to final moulding. The protein or gluten in wheat flour is highly elastic after rounding and may break if insufficient rest is given. The result is a loaf with rough texture and low volume.

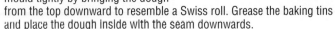

From front: Malt Bread, Wheat Germ Bread.

Bloomers

Ingredients:

Plain flour (all-purpose flour)	125 g
Strong white flour (bread flour)	375 g
Malt flour	10 g
Milk powder	5 g
Bread improver	8 g
Instant dry yeast	8 g
Salt	10 g
Cold water	330 g
Shortening	10 g

Method:

- With an electric mixer and dough hook at low speed, blend the dry ingredients together for about 1 minute. Add cold water and continue mixing on low speed for another minute. Put in shortening and mix on medium speed for 12 minutes until dough is fully developed.

- Transfer the dough onto a flour-dusted work surface and round up the dough with both hands. Place dough into an airtight container and let it rise in a warm place for 1 hour until dough is double in bulk.

- Divide dough into 2 pieces 420 g each and mould round. Leave for 10 minutes. Remould the dough pieces and form each piece into a long baton shape. Prove in a warm, draught-free place for 1–1¹/₂ hours. Make 7 cuts, each 1-cm deep across the top of each dough piece.

- Preheat the oven to 230°C. Bake with a tray of water to generate steam for the first 10 minutes of the baking time. Open the door of the oven and remove any water remaining. Continue to bake for 10–15 minutes. Cool on a wire rack.

French Baguette

Ingredients:

Strong white flour (bread flour)	500 g
Bread improver	7 g
Instant dry yeast	7 g
Salt	10 g
Cold water	330 g

Method:

- With an electric mixer and dough hook at low speed, blend the dry ingredients together for about 1 minute. Add water and mix on low speed for another minute. Increase to medium speed and mix for 12 minutes until dough is fully developed.

- Transfer the dough onto a flour-dusted work surface and round up dough with both hands. Place the dough into an airtight container and let it rise in a warm place for 1–1¹/₂ hours until dough is double in bulk.

- Divide the dough into 4 pieces, each weighing 200 g. Round up the dough and leave for 15 minutes. Mould each dough piece into a cylindrical shape 30 cm long. Do this by flattening the dough with a rolling pin and then rolling the dough tightly from one end downwards, making certain that the seam is properly sealed.

- Transfer the dough pieces onto a lightly greased, perforated tray and prove in a warm, draught-free place for 1¹/₂–2 hours. When the dough is ready, make 3 diagonal cuts on the surface of each dough piece, using a sharp knife. Space the cuts 10 cm apart.

- Preheat the oven to 230°C. Bake with a tray of water to generate steam for the first 10 minutes of the baking time. Open the door of the oven and remove any water remaining. Continue to bake for about 10 minutes until the bread is golden brown.

Chef's Tip:

Lean dough or dough made without fat or sugar is best baked in an oven with steam. The steam treatment can be improvised by putting a tray filled with about ¹/₂ cm of water into the oven when preheating the oven. The presence of steam during the first half of baking creates a moist atmosphere that allows full expansion of the dough. The result is a thin, glossy and crispy crust with an improved volume.

Chef's Tip:

This recipe is also suitable for making coburgs. To make coburgs, the dough is shaped round and given 2 cuts making a cross.

From left: Bloomers, French Baguette.

French Country Bread

Ingredients:

Sponge

Strong flour (bread flour)	350 g
Instant dry yeast	4 g
Cold water	210 g

Dough

Strong flour (bread flour)	100 g
Rye flour	25 g
Wheat bran	25 g
Bread improver	8 g
Instant dry yeast	3 g
Salt	10 g
Water	110 g
Butter	10 g

Method:

- With an electric mixer and dough hook, prepare the sponge by mixing the 3 ingredients on slow speed for 3 minutes. The sponge should be firm, dry and cool (24°C) to the touch. Ferment the sponge for 4–5 hours in an airtight container at about 27°C.

- When the sponge is ready, prepare the dough. Place the remaining dry ingredients into the mixer. Add water and mix on low speed. Immediately cut sponge into a few pieces and add to the mixture over 1 minute. Increase to medium speed and mix for 2 minutes. Add butter and mix for another 7–10 minutes until dough is fully developed.

- Round up and leave dough for 10 minutes. Divide the dough into 2 pieces, each 420 g and round up. Leave for another 10 minutes and round up to expel any carbon dioxide gas generated during fermentation

- Place the dough pieces onto a greased baking tray and let it rise in a warm place (37°C) for 1–1½ hours. When the dough pieces have doubled in size, make a few cuts on the surface to create a nice design.

- Preheat the oven to 230°C. Bake with a tray of water to generate for the first 12 minutes of baking time. Open the door of the oven briefly to release the steam and remove any water remaining. Continue to bake for another 8–10 minutes.

After mixing, the sponge must be cool and dry. During fermentation, the gluten in the flour will be restructured for better gas retention. The fermentation time can be extended or shortened by reducing or increasing the amount of yeast proportionally. The sponge is matured when its volume is 3 times its original size.

Tiger Bread

Ingredients:

Sponge

Strong white flour (bread flour)	350 g
Instant dry yeast	4 g
Water	210 g

Dough

Strong white flour (bread flour)	150 g
Milk powder	8 g
Bread improver	8 g
Instant dry yeast	5 g
Salt	10 g
Water	100 g
Shortening	5 g

Method:

- With an electric mixer and dough hook, prepare the sponge by mixing the 3 ingredients on low speed for 3 minutes. The sponge should be firm, dry and cool (24°C) to the touch. Ferment the sponge for 4–5 hours in an airtight container at about 27°C.

- When the sponge is ready, prepare the dough. Place the remaining dry ingredients into the mixer, add water and mix on low speed. Immediately cut the sponge into a few pieces and add to the mixture over 1 minute. Increase to medium speed and mix for 2 minutes. Add shortening and mix for another 5–7 minutes until the dough is fully developed.

- Round up and leave the dough for 10 minutes. Divide it into 2 pieces, each 420 g and mould round. Leave for another 10 minutes. Remould the dough pieces into a long baton shape and place onto a lightly greased tray.

- Prove in a warm place for 1–1½ hours. After proving, brush 40–50 g of Tiger Paste (*see recipe*) onto the top of the dough.

- Preheat the oven to 230°C. Bake with a tray of water to generate steam for 10 minutes. Open the door of the oven to release steam and remove any water remaining. Continue to bake for 10–15 minutes. Cool on a wire rack.

To improve the crust, dust the tray with semolina or sugi flour before putting the dough on it. If the fermented tiger paste is too thick, thin it down with some water. A paste with the right consistency will result in a decorative surface that will crack and colour beautifully during baking.

From front: Tiger Bread, French Country Bread.

Tiger Paste

Ingredients:

Yeast	2 g
Warm water	50 g
Sugar	3 g
Cooking oil	3 g
Rice flour	50 g
Salt	1 g

Method:

- Disperse the yeast in warm water (37°C) then add sugar. Stir the mixture to dissolve the sugar. Add cooking oil and mix with a hand whisk. Add rice flour and mix to a paste.

- Ferment the paste for 30 minutes before using.

Cream Cheese Nut Roll

Ingredients:
Sponge

Strong flour (bread flour)	420 g
Instant dry yeast	4 g
Water	250 g

Dough

Strong flour (bread flour)	30 g
Plain flour (all purpose flour)	150 g
Milk powder	30 g
Bread improver	7 g
Instant dry yeast	12 g
Sugar	120 g
Salt	9 g
Eggs	90 g (2, small), chilled
Butter	90 g
Cream cheese filling*	
Raisins	200 g
Walnuts	200g, toasted

Method:

- With an electric mixer and dough hook, prepare the sponge by mixing the three ingredients on slow speed for 3 minutes. The sponge should be firm, dry and cool (24°C) to the touch. Ferment the sponge for 4–5 hours in an airtight container at about 27°C.

- When the sponge is ready, prepare the dough. Place the remaining dry ingredients into the mixer, add chilled eggs and begin to mix on slow speed. Immediately cut sponge into a few pieces and add to the mixture over 1 minute. Increase speed to medium and mix for 2 minutes. Add butter and mix for another 7–10 minutes. Round up the dough and leave on flour-dusted work surface for 15 minutes.

- Roll out the dough into a 1-cm thick rectangular sheet, measuring 30 cm by 50 cm. Spread cream cheese filling (*see recipe*) over the entire surface of the dough and sprinkle raisins and walnuts over it.

- Roll the dough up lengthwise like a Swiss roll and apply water on the seam to seal well. Brush melted butter all over the dough and cut into 12 pieces. Arrange the slices in 3 rows of 4 in a 6-cm high baking tray, measuring 30 cm by 40 cm.

- Leave to prove in a warm place for 1 hour until the dough doubles in size. Brush the surface with egg and sprinkle with sliced almond (or almond flakes). Bake in a preheated oven at 190°C for 25–30 minutes until golden brown.

*Cream Cheese Filling

Ingredients:

Cream cheese	500 g
Sugar	200 g
Egg	50 g, (1, small)
Plain flour	115 g
Raisins	60 g

Method:

- Using a paddle, beat cream cheese and sugar on medium speed for 3 minutes until well blended. Add egg gradually and mix on medium speed for another 2 minutes. Fold in the flour and raisins on slow speed for 1 minute.

- Store in the refrigerator until needed.

 Chef's Tip: As a variation to this recipe, add coffee paste and instant coffee powder to the cream cheese filling to make cappuccino cream cheese rolls. Similarly, add cocoa and chocolate paste to the filling for chocolate cream cheese rolls.

Pizza Base (Wholemeal)

Ingredients:

Strong white flour (bread flour)	425 g
Wheat bran	75 g
Milk powder	15 g
Bread improver	7 g
Instant dry yeast	9 g
Sugar	10 g
Salt	10 g
Cold water	330 g
Butter	25 g

Method:

- With an electric mixer and dough hook at low speed, blend the dry ingredients together for 1–2 minutes. Add water and continue mixing on low speed for 2 minutes. Put in butter and mix on medium speed for 12–15 minutes until the dough is fully developed.

- Transfer the dough onto a flour-dusted work surface and round up the dough with both hands. Place the dough into an airtight container and let it rise in a warm place for 1 hour until the dough is double in bulk.

- Divide the dough into 9 pieces, each 100 g. Round up and leave for 15 minutes. Press down and roll the dough pieces round with a rolling pin. Prick the dough pieces with a fork to prevent the centre of the dough from rising during proving.

- Prove the dough pieces for 20–30 minutes in a warm, draught-free room. Bake in a preheated oven at 225°C for 10–12 minutes until the dough has a slight colour. Spread pizza topping over the dough and sprinkle some parmesan cheese.

- To make Hawaiian pizza, garnish with diced pineapple, roast chicken, mushrooms, onions, green and red peppers. Finish off with a blend of mozzarella and cheddar cheese on top. Bake in a preheated oven at 225°C for 10–12 minutes until the cheese turns slightly brown.

Chef's Tip:
Dusting the table with a little flour and flipping the dough around after each rolling will result in a round pizza. You can also roll out the dough to 0.5-cm thickness and cut with a round cutter.

Pizza Topping

Ingredients:

Ripe tomatoes	700 g
Cooking oil	35 g
Shallots	8 g, chopped
Garlic	6 g, chopped
Bay leaf	3 pieces
Onions	100 g
Tomato paste	150 g
Sugar	20 g
Salt	6 g
Oregano	2 g
Ground black pepper	6 g

Method:

- With a sharp knife, make a cross at the bottom of the ripe tomatoes. Blanch the tomatoes in boiling water for 15 minutes until the skin can be easily removed. Discard the skin, core and seeds but retain the fleshy part of the tomatoes. Put into the food processor and puree the tomatoes.

- In a frying pan, add oil and fry chopped shallots, garlic and bay leaf until it turns yellowish. Add onions and fry for 10 minutes to dry up the onions. Pour in the tomato paste and the fresh tomato puree and fry for 20 minutes until the sauce starts to thicken. Season with sugar, salt, oregano and black pepper and cook for another 10 minutes.

Philippines Bread

Ingredients:

Strong white flour (bread flour)	400 g
Plain flour (all purpose flour)	100 g
Bread improver	8 g
Instant dry yeast	10 g
Sugar'	100 g
Salt	8 g
Egg	50 g (1, small)
Cold water	200 g
Butter	60 g

Method:

* With an electric mixer and dough hook at low speed, blend the dry ingredients together for 1 minute. Add egg then water and mix on low speed for 2 minutes. Add butter and continue to mix for another 3 minutes on low speed. The dough is slightly stiff and underdeveloped at this stage.

* Place dough into an airtight container and let it rise in a warm place for 1 hour.

* Dust flour on work surface and roll out the dough. Fold dough into 2, turn 90°C and roll out again. Repeat this process at least 8 times with a few minutes in between the folds until the dough is smooth and fully developed. Leave for 15 minutes.

* Roll out the dough into a 4-mm thick sheet and cut into triangles 1-cm wide at the base and 2-cm long. Roll up from the base to the tip to resemble a croissant. Allow the dough to prove for about 1 hour until the dough is doubled in size.

* Brush the tops with egg glaze and bake in a preheated oven at 200°C for 12–15 minutes until glossy and golden brown. Turn out and cool on a wire rack.

Steamed Slice Roll

Ingredients:

Plain flour (all-purpose flour)	500 g
Baking powder	8 g
Instant dry yeast	4 g
Sugar	50 g
Cold water	250 g
Shortening	35 g

Method:

* With an electric mixer and dough hook at low speed, blend the dry ingredients together for about 1 minute. Add water and mix on low speed for 2 minutes. Put in shortening and mix on medium speed for 6 minutes until the dough is half developed.

* Leave for 10 minutes and roll out. Fold into half and roll out again. Repeat this 6–8 times until the dough is smooth. Leave dough for another 10 minutes and divide into 2. Roll out 1 piece into a rectangular shape about 0.5-cm thick and cut into strips. Roll the other dough piece into a thin sheet and wrap it around the length of 8–10 strips of dough. The two ends of the dough strips should be exposed.

* Arrange the rolls in a steamer and leave it to prove for 1–1½ hours. Steam the proved rolls on high heat for 12–15 minutes.

Chef's Tip:
It is necessary to use cold water for this recipe in order to control the fermentation process. This will produce a less sticky and more manageable dough.

Chef's Tip:
The surface can be brushed with evaporated milk instead of egg to give it a nice finish. If a chewy bread is desired, the bread can be baked at three-quarters prove. Rolling and folding the dough repeatedly creates bread with a fine grain and texture.

From front: Philippines Bread, Steamed Slice Roll.

Red Bean Pau

Ingredients:

Plain flour (all-purpose flour)	300 g
Baking powder	15 g
Milk powder	6 g
Instant dry yeast	9 g
Sugar	90 g
Salt	2 g
Cold water	145 g
Shortening	30 g
Red bean paste*	350 g

Method:

- With an electric mixer and dough hook at low speed, blend the dry ingredients together for about 1 minute. Add water and mix on low speed for 2 minutes. Put in shortening and mix on medium speed for 6 minutes until the dough is half developed.

- Transfer the dough onto a flour-dusted work surface and round up. Leave the dough to ferment for 30–40 minutes and roll out. Fold into half and roll out again. Repeat this 6–8 times until the dough is smooth.

- Leave dough for 15 minutes and divide into 40 g pieces. Round up and leave dough pieces for another 10 minutes.

- Roll out each piece of dough round with the edges thinner than the centre. Place 25 g of red bean paste in the centre and pleat the dough from the edges to the centre. With the seam facing downwards, stick a square greaseproof paper on it.

- Arrange the paus at least 2.5 cm apart on a steaming tray and prove for 30 minutes. Steam on high heat for 12–15 minutes.

* Red bean paste is readily available at baking specialty stores.

This recipe is easy and takes a short time to prepare. However, due to the short fermentation time, it is advisable to consume the buns as soon as possible after cooking. Steaming the buns prior to consumption produces the best eating quality. Warming up the buns in the microwave should be avoided as the process toughens and dries up the bun.

Barbecue Chicken Pau

Ingredients:

Plain flour (all-purpose flour)	500 g
Baking powder	15 g
Instant dry yeast	10 g
Sugar	110 g
Cold water	230 g
Shortening	30 g
Barbecue Chicken Filling*	

Method:

- With an electric mixer and dough hook at low speed, blend the dry ingredients together for about 1 minute. Add water and mix on low speed for another minute. Put in shortening and mix on medium speed for 6 minutes until the dough is half developed.

- Transfer the dough onto a flour-dusted work surface and round up. Rest the dough for 10 minutes and roll out. Fold in half and roll out again. Repeat this 6–8 times until the dough is smooth.

- Leave for 15 minutes and divide into 40 g pieces. Round up and leave the dough pieces for another 10 minutes. Roll out each piece of dough into rounds with the edges thinner than the centre. Place 30 g of barbecue chicken filling (*see recipe*) in the centre and pleat the dough from the edges to the centre. Place the pau on small square pieces of greaseproof paper.

- Arrange the pau at least 1 inch apart in a steamer and steam on high heat for 12–15 minutes.

The water in the steamer must be boiling when placing the pau into the steamer. The steamer cover must be tightly closed and it must not be opened during the first 12 minutes of steaming. A high-pressure gas stove will produce pau with better volume and a softer texture.

Clockwise from right: Barbecue Chicken Pau, Red Bean Pau, Barbecue Chicken Pau.

*Barbecue Chicken Filling

Ingredients:

Chicken	100 g, cut in strips
Chinese wine	9 g
Garlic	6 g, chopped

Marinade:

Salt	4 g
Monosodium glutamate (MSG)	6 g
Sugar	12 g
Ground white pepper	2 g
Plum sauce	8 g
Sesame oil	9 g
Water	15 g
Dark soy sauce	3 g
Oyster sauce	6 g

Savoury Paste:

Sesame oil	15 g
Onion	5 g (small)
Spring onion	5 g
Ginger	5 g, chopped
Water	30 g
Dark soy sauce	11 g
Light soy sauce	7 g
Monosodium glutamate (MSG)	7 g

Sugar	40 g
Oyster sauce	28 g
Ground white pepper	12 g
Tapioca flour	12 g
Corn flour	12 g
Water	160 g

Method:

- Season the chicken strips with wine and garlic. In a separate bowl, combine the marinade ingredients. Place the chicken strips into the bowl of marinade and refrigerate for a few hours. Place marinated chicken strips in a baking tray and bake at 200°C for 25–30 minutes until cooked. Cut into 1-cm cubes.

- To make the savoury paste, heat sesame oil in a wok and fry the small onion, spring onion and ginger until brown. Add 30 g of water and bring the mixture to a boil. Strain to remove the onion, spring onion and ginger.

- In another bowl, mix the rest of the ingredients except tapioca flour, corn flour and 160 g water together and add to the stock. Cook on low heat for a few minutes.

- Mix the tapioca flour and corn flour with 160 g water to form a paste. Add to the stock and cook for 1 minute until it thickens into a paste. Add the barbecue chicken cubes to the paste, mix well and chill before using.

Fried Steamed Roll

Ingredients:

Sponge

Plain flour (all-purpose flour)	120 g
Instant dry yeast	2 g
Water	65 g

Dough

Plain flour (all-purpose flour)	180 g
Baking powder	8 g
Ammonium bicarbonate	2 g
Sugar	40 g
Egg white	40 g
Cold water	60 g
Shortening	20 g

Method:

- With an electric mixer and dough hook, prepare the sponge by mixing the 3 ingredients on low speed for 3–4 minutes. Ferment sponge for 3–4 hours in an airtight container at about 27°C.

- Prepare the dough by combining the sponge with the rest of the ingredients except for the shortening and mix for 2 minutes on low speed. Add the shortening and mix on medium speed for 6 minutes until dough is half developed.

- Transfer the dough onto a flour-dusted work surface and round up. Leave dough for 10 minutes and roll out. Fold into 2 and roll out again. Repeat this 6–8 times until the dough is smooth. Leave dough for 15 minutes and divide into 50 g pieces. Round up and leave dough pieces for another 10 minutes.

- Roll out each dough piece to a length of 15 cm. Brush lightly with oil and fold into a semi-circle. With a metal scrapper, make 6–8 cuts about 5 cm long and 0.5 cm apart on the folded edge of the semi-circle. Open up the dough and twist the two ends in opposite directions. Loop the twisted dough and tuck one end underneath to form a snail-like shape. Place the dough on a square of greaseproof paper and leave to prove for 30 minutes.

- Steam for 12–15 minutes and deep fry in a wok of hot oil (180°C) till golden brown. Glaze with honey and sprinkle with toasted sesame seeds if desired.

 Ammonium bicarbonate is a leavening agent that improves the volume of the dough.

Butterfly Steamed Bun

Ingredients:

Sponge

Plain flour (all-purpose flour)	200 g
Instant dry yeast	3 g
Water	110 g

Dough

Plain flour (all-purpose flour)	300 g
Baking powder	15 g
Sugar	150 g
Cold water	140 g
Shortening	15 g

Method:

- With an electric mixer and dough hook, prepare the sponge by mixing the 3 ingredients on low speed for 3–4 minutes. Leave sponge to rise for 3–4 hours in an airtight container at about 27°C.

- Prepare the dough by mixing the sponge with the rest of the ingredients except shortening for 2 minutes on low speed. Add shortening and mix on medium speed for 6 minutes until dough is half developed.

- Transfer the dough onto a flour-dusted work surface and round up. Leave dough for 10 minutes and roll out. Fold into 2 and roll out again. Repeat this for 6–8 times until the dough is smooth. Leave for 15 minutes. Divide into 30 g portions, round up and leave for another 10 minutes.

- Roll out each portion of the dough into a circle with the edges thinner than the centre. Brush lightly with oil and fold to form a semi-circle. With a metal scrapper, make a 1-cm long cut in the centre of the semi-circle.

- Press the base of the semi-circle with your thumb and index finger to shape the butterfly's head. Make an imprint on each side of the cut to represent the wings. Using food colouring, put dots on each side of the butterfly's head to form the eyes.

- Arrange on a lightly greased metal tray and place in the steamer. Prove for 30 minutes and steam on high heat for 12–15 minutes.

Rolling and folding the dough many times produces a dough with good colour and texture. It may be necessary to rest the dough for 10 minutes after several times of rolling and folding so as not to tear the gluten matrix.

From front: Fried Steamed Roll, Butterfly Steamed Bun.

Hot Cross Bun

Ingredients:

Strong white flour (bread flour)	400 g
Plain flour (all-purpose flour)	100 g
Milk powder	10 g
Bread improver	8 g
Instant dry yeast	15 g
Ground cinnamon	5 g
Ground ginger	3 g
Mixed spice	2 g
Ground nutmeg	1 g
Sugar	55 g
Salt	5 g
Egg	25 g (½, small)
Cold water	295 g
Butter	55 g, softened
Raisins	150 g
Orange peel	25 g

Method:

- With an electric mixer and dough hook at low speed, blend the dry ingredients together for 1 minute. Add egg then water and mix on low speed for another minute. Increase to medium speed and mix for 5 minutes. Add butter and continue mixing for 7–10 minutes. Mix in raisins and orange peel on low speed over 1 minute making sure not to crush the raisins.

- Transfer the dough onto a flour-dusted work surface and round up the dough with both hands. Place the dough into an airtight container and let it rise in a warm place for 1 hour until the dough doubles in size.

- Divide the dough into 80 g pieces. Mould the dough pieces into balls and let them rest for 10 minutes. Round up the dough pieces again and place on a greased baking tray. Prove the dough pieces for 1 hour in a warm, draught-free room until the dough doubles in size.

- Line the dough pieces side by side on a baking tray. Brush beaten egg over the surface and pipe straight lines over buns with the crossing mixture (*see recipe*), making a cross on each piece.

- Bake in a preheated oven at 200°C for 15–20 minutes. Immediately after removing from oven, brush bun glaze or sugar syrup over the buns to give them a glossy finish.

Crossing Mixture

Ingredients:

Plain flour (all-purpose) flour	300 g
Milk powder	35 g
Baking powder	2 g
Shortening	65 g
Salt	2 g
Water	320 g

- Mix all the ingredients together, adding water slowly to avoid creating lumps.

Chef's Tip: Spices have a retarding effect on yeast fermentation. If you prefer to increase the amount of spice in the recipe, the fermentation and proving time may need to be extended by 10–20 minutes.

Braided Challah

Ingredients:

Strong white flour (bread flour)	500 g
Bread improver	8 g
Instant dry yeast	11 g
Sugar	40 g
Salt	10 g
Water	150 g
Eggs	125 g (2, large)
Butter	50 g, softened

Topping
Sesame seeds

Method:

- With an electric mixer and dough hook, mix the dry ingredients for 1 minute on low speed. Add water and eggs and mix on low speed for another minute. Increase to medium speed for 3 minutes. Add butter and mix for another 10 minutes until dough is fully developed.

- Round up dough and place into an airtight container to rise in a warm place for 1 hour until dough is double in bulk. Divide the dough into 50 g pieces. Round up the pieces and leave for 10 minutes.

- To braid a loaf, take 6 portions and roll each into a 20-cm long strip. Each strip should be thinner at the ends and thicker in the middle. Place all the 6 strips with the tips at one end touching. Weave the strips together to form a braid.

- Prove the braid in a warm place for about 1 hour. Brush beaten egg over the surface and sprinkle sesame seeds over the dough if desired. Bake in a preheated oven at 200°C for 20–25 minutes.

Chef's Tip: To make a 6 strand braid, first place strip 6 over strip 1 (once and not repeated). Weave strip 2 over strip 6, 1 over 3, 5 over 1 and 6 over 4. This is repeated until the braid is completed.

Panetonne

Ingredients:

Sponge

Strong flour (bread flour)	250 g
Instant dry yeast	4 g
Water	150 g

Dough

Strong flour (bread flour)	250 g
Milk powder	25 g
Bread improver	8 g
Instant dry yeast	10 g
Sugar	60 g
Salt	5 g
Eggs	130 g (2, medium)
Sugar syrup	40 g
Vanilla flavouring	3 g
Orange flavouring	3 g
Lemon flavouring	3 g
Butter	100 g
Raisins	200 g
Glazed red cherries	50 g

Method:

- With an electric mixer and dough hook, prepare the sponge by mixing flour, yeast and cold water on low speed for 3 minutes. The sponge should be firm, dry and cool (24°C) to the touch. Ferment the sponge for 4–5 hours in an airtight container at about 27°C.

- When the sponge is ready, prepare the dough. Place the remaining dry ingredients into the mixer with eggs, sugar syrup and flavouring. Immediately cut the sponge into a few pieces and add to the above mixture over 2 minutes on low speed.

- Increase speed to medium and mix for 2 minutes. Add butter and mix for another 7–10 minutes until dough is fully developed. Mix in raisins and glazed cherries on low speed for 1 minute until well blended.

- Round up the dough and leave for 10 minutes. Divide the dough into 120 g pieces and mould into balls. Leave to rest for another 10 minutes. Round up the dough pieces again and place in special panettone paper cups about 5-cm deep and 5-cm wide.

- Prove the dough for 1 hour in a warm place. Brush with beaten egg and cut a cross on the surface with scissors and sprinkle sugar. Bake in a preheated oven at 190°C for 20–25 minutes.

Chef's Tip:

To prepare sugar syrup, cook 3 parts (450 g) of sugar with 1 part (150 g) of water on low heat for 25 minutes. Add a piece of lime cut into quarters into the syrup during cooking to prevent the sugar from crystallizing on cooling. After the first 15 minutes of baking, it is advisable to put an aluminium foil over the tops of the panetonne to prevent excessive browning.

Stollen

Ingredients:

Raisins	225 g
Orange peel	150 g
Sugar syrup	30 g
Dark rum	30 g

Ferment

Strong flour (bread flour)	100 g
Instant dry yeast	15 g
Milk	150 g, warmed to 38°C

Dough

Strong flour (bread flour)	200 g
Plain flour (all purpose flour)	100 g
Bread improver	8 g
Sugar	45 g
Salt	4 g
Ground almond	45 g
Marzipan	75 g
Allspice	7 g
Egg	60 g (1, large), chilled
Butter	120 g

Method:

- Combine raisins, orange peel, sugar syrup and rum and soak overnight at room temperature.

- Prepare ferment by combining flour, yeast and milk together. Ferment for 30 minutes.

- To prepare the dough, place the remaining dry ingredients into the mixer. Add ferment and cold egg and begin to mix on low speed. Increase speed to medium and mix for 2 minutes. Add butter and mix for another 7–10 minutes until the dough is fully developed. Mix in the raisins and orange peel mixture on low speed for 1 minute until well blended.

- Place the dough in a lightly greased container, cover, and let it rise for 1 hour until doubled in bulk. Turn dough out onto flour-dusted work surface. Divide the dough into 4 pieces, each 350 g. Round up the dough pieces and leave for 15 minutes.

- Roll out each dough piece into a round shape and fold in half. Prove the dough pieces for 45 minutes in a warm place until the dough increases by two thirds its original size.

- Bake in a preheated oven at 180°C for 30 minutes or until golden brown. When cool, brush with melted butter and coat with icing sugar.

Several coats of butter can be applied to the stollen to give it moisture and an extra rich taste. A roll of marzipan can also be folded into the dough prior to proving.

glossary

1. **Oat bran:** This is outer casing of the oat kernel and is high in fibre. It is relatively thin and pale in colour, compared to wheat bran.

2. **Rye flour:** Rye flour contains less protein (gluten) than wheat flour and is often combined with the latter to make bread. Rye flour is dark and dense and produces bread that keeps moist for a longer period of time than wheat bread.

3. **Bread flour:** A special blend of high protein flour usually milled from hard winter wheat.

4. **Dry wheat gluten:** Also known as gluten flour, dry wheat gluten is high protein flour that has been treated to remove most of its starch content. It is added to specialty breads like multigrain bread because of the high percentage of seeds and nuts used.

5. **Bread improver:** Often referred to as a dough conditioner, bread improver is a balanced mixture of ingredients designed to modify gluten and improve gas production and finished product quality.

6. **Multigrain:** A mixture of different types of seeds and grains such as millet, barley bran, rice bran, sesame seeds, poppy seeds, rolled oats, flaxseeds, pumpkin seeds and sunflower seeds. It is used to give colour, flavour and texture to bread.

7. **Celery powder:** Prepared from ground celery seeds, celery powder is used to enhance the flavour of bread.

8. **Ammonium bicarbonate:** A leavening agent that releases ammonia gas and carbon dioxide.

9. **Wheat bran:** The hard outer covering of wheat kernel. It is high in fibre and vitamin B and is usually added to bread for additional flavour.

10. **Malt flour:** A flour containing maltose sugar, extracted from sprouted barley or wheat. It is a nutritious additive to breads.

11. **Calcium propionate:** An antimicrobial mould inhibitor used in processed foods such as baked goods, cheeses, jams and jellies.

12. **Yeast:** A microscopic fungus that can ferment simple sugars into carbon dioxide gas and alcohol. There are three main types; fresh yeast, active dry yeast and instant dry yeast. Fresh yeast has a short shelf life and requires refrigeration. Dry yeast is complicated to use, requiring re-hydration in warm water for 15 minutes. Instant dry yeast can be blended directly into flour, has long shelf life and good gassing power.

13. **All-purpose flour:** General-purpose flour often referred to as medium protein flour. It is ideal for making cookies, pies and pastries.

14. **Wheat germ:** The embryo of the wheat kernel, wheat germ is high in fats and rich in vitamins, proteins and minerals. It is usually removed during milling because it contains fats which limits the keeping quality of flour.

15. **Superfine flour:** Also known as high ratio flour, this is low protein flour milled to fine even-sized granules and treated to make it suitable for caking-making.

16. **White sesame seeds:** These tiny flat seeds of a plant (*Sesamum indicum*) native to India have a nutty and slightly sweet flavour. They are often sprinkled on top of bread doughs and buns, as they are delicious when baked.

glossary

20

24

28

32

17. **Shortening:** A white, flavourless, solid vegetable fat formulated mainly for baking. It is used as a tenderiser in bread and flour products.

18. **Chocolate chips:** Couvature chocolate chips are a finely milled and conched mixture of cocoa butter, cocoa powder and sugar, made into small chips about 7 mm in size. For compound chocolate chips, cocoa butter is replaced with hydrogenated palm kernel oil. It is used to enhance the taste and presentation of baked products.

19. **Icing sugar:** Also known as confectioner's sugar and powdered sugar, these finely powdered sugar crystals are usually used for decorating baking goods.

20. **Almond flakes:** The sliced nut of the almond tree, almond flakes impart a distinctive flavour, aroma and attractive appearance to baked products.

21. **Prunes:** Dried red or purple plums, prunes can be eaten straight from the pack or used in sweet and savoury dishes.

22. **Brown sugar:** Made from cane sugar, brown sugar has a coating of molasses which give it its characteristic flavour and colour.

23. **Honey:** A sweet, viscous liquid made by bees from flower nectar, honey is natural sugar syrup. It imparts good flavour and helps to retain moisture when used in baked goods.

24. **Desiccated coconut:** Dehydrated finely grated coconut. It is usually used to add texture to baked goods.

25. **Cream cheese:** Also known as bakers' cheese, it is popularly used for making fillings for Danish pastries and in the manufacture of cheesecakes and mousses. It provides richness and flavour to baked products.

26. **Parmesan cheese:** A hard, dry cheese made from skimmed milk. It has a distinctive flavour and is usually grated and used to flavour foods.

27. **Mozzarella cheese:** Elastic and stringy, this cheese originally made from buffalo milk. But now it is made mostly from cow's milk. It is used to add texture rather than a specific taste to a dish.

28. **Cheddar cheese:** A firm cheese made from cow's milk. It ranges from mild to strong in flavour and from white to orange in colour.

29. **Castor sugar:** These fine sugar crystals are commonly used to sweeten foods, including liquids and baked goods.

30. **Raisins:** A sweet dried grape, raisins provide taste and sweetness to baked products.

31. **Butter:** Made from milk fat, butter has a highly desirable flavour. Butter absorbs flavours readily and should be wrapped tightly when stored in the refrigerator.

32. **Treacle:** A sweet, dark-coloured by-product of the sugar refining process, treacle is used to impart colour and flavour to baked products.

weights & measures

Quantities for this book are given in Metric and American (spoon and cup) measures. Standard spoon and cup measurements used are: 1 tsp = 5 ml, 1 dsp = 10 ml, 1 Tbsp = 15 ml, 1 cup = 250 ml.
All measures are level unless otherwise stated.

LIQUID AND VOLUME MEASURES

Metric	Imperial	American
5 ml	1/6 fl oz	1 tsp
10 ml	1/3 fl oz	1 dsp
15 ml	1/2 fl oz	1 Tbsp
60 ml	2 fl oz	1/4 cup (4 Tbsp)
85 ml	2 1/2 fl oz	1/3 cup
90 ml	3 fl oz	3/8 cup (6 Tbsp)
125 ml	4 fl oz	1/2 cup
180 ml	6 fl oz	3/4 cup
250 ml	8 fl oz	1 cup
300 ml	10 fl oz (1/2 pint)	1 1/4 cups
375 ml	12 fl oz	1 1/2 cups
435 ml	14 fl oz	1 3/4 cups
500 ml	16 fl oz	2 cups
625 ml	20 fl oz (1 pint)	2 1/2 cups
750 ml	24 fl oz (1 1/5 pints)	3 cups
1 litre	32 fl oz (1 3/5 pints)	4 cups
1.25 litres	40 fl oz (2 pints)	5 cups
1.5 litres	48 fl oz (2 2/5 pints)	6 cups
2.5 litres	80 fl oz (4 pints)	10 cups

DRY MEASURES

Metric	Imperial
30 g	1 ounce
45 g	1 1/2 ounces
55 g	2 ounces
70 g	2 1/2 ounces
85 g	3 ounces
100 g	3 1/2 ounces
110 g	4 ounces
125 g	4 1/2 ounces
140 g	5 ounces
280 g	10 ounces
450 g	16 ounces (1 pound)
500 g	1 pound, 1 1/2 ounces
700 g	1 1/2 pounds
800 g	1 3/4 pounds
1 kg	2 pounds, 3 ounces
1.5 kg	3 pounds, 4 1/2 ounces
2 kg	4 pounds, 6 ounces

OVEN TEMPERATURE

	°C	°F	Gas Regulo
Very slow	120	250	1
Slow	150	300	2
Moderately slow	160	325	3
Moderate	180	350	4
Moderately hot	190/200	370/400	5/6
Hot	210/220	410/440	6/7
Very hot	230	450	8
Super hot	250/290	475/550	9/10

LENGTH

Metric	Imperial
0.5 cm	1/4 inch
1 cm	1/2 inch
1.5 cm	3/4 inch
2.5 cm	1 inch